A Brief History of
Rhinebeck
NANCY KELLY

All proceeds from the sale of this book
will go to the Historical Society.

The cover illustration is a detail from the mural
in the Rhinebeck Post Office painted by Olin Dows.

Cover design by Chloe Alexander.

THE WISE FAMILY TRUST
in cooperation with
Historical Society of Rhinebeck

Acknowledgements

I am very grateful for the generous funding from the Wise Family Trust which has enabled this publication, allowing us update Dewitt Gurnell's "Condensed History of Rhinebeck" in a more complete manner. Mr. Robert Wise conceived the idea and has been assisted by his informal local representative, Herman Gorgens in smoothing the pathway toward publication. A special thanks goes to Duke Vicks of Vicks Lithograph and Printing Corporation. Many of the photos and details for the history have been located through the use of a database prepared by the Consortium of Rhinebeck History funded by the Thomas Thompson Trust. This catalog of historical material is becoming ever more useful as it nears completion.

Kay Verrilli, editor of the picture captions for the 1990 Tercentennial publication, "Portrait of a Town," has been particularly helpful in locating photos and sharing time and knowledge. Readers should refer to this book by Sari Tietjen for broader coverage of many of these topics.

It is difficult to name all those who have assisted me. They include Ada Harrison, curator of the Museum of Rhinebeck History and Regent of the Chancellor Livingston Chapter, NSDAR, Marilyn Hatch of the Quitman Resource Center for Preservation with her work on the Rhinebeck National Register Survey, and also Nick McCausland of the Rhinebeck Historical Society, local historians, Barbara Frost and Mary Frazer and Red Hook Historian, J. Winthrop Aldrich. A special word of thanks should go to my husband Arthur Kelly, whose meticulous work in transcribing and indexing early area records has done much to facilitate the study of genealogy and history in our area. His knowledge and patience with this project have been invaluable.

Project manager and interior design:
Len Vogler

US International Standard Book Number: 0-8256-9423-X

Reorder from:
THE WISE FAMILY TRUST
257 Park Avenue South
New York, NY 10010

printed in the United States of America by
Vicks Lithograph and Printing Corporation

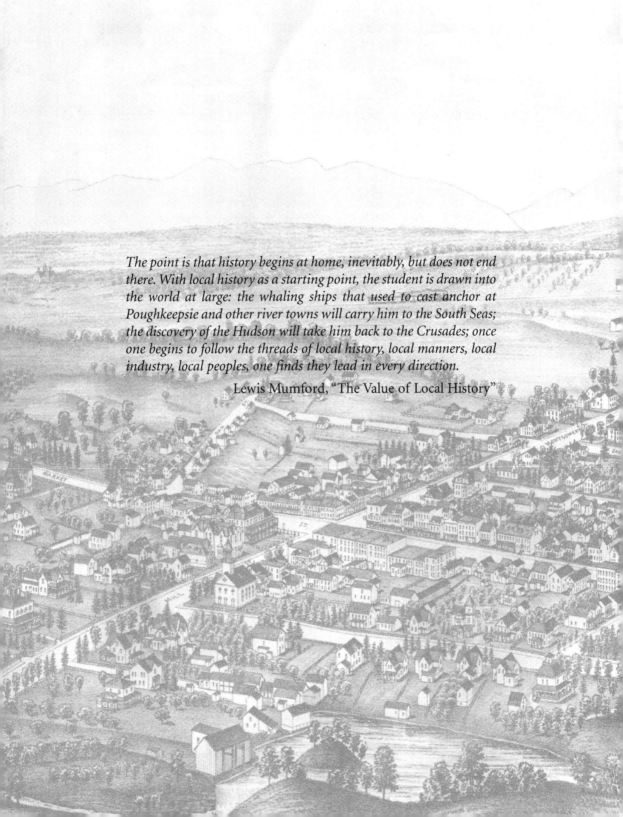

The point is that history begins at home, inevitably, but does not end there. With local history as a starting point, the student is drawn into the world at large: the whaling ships that used to cast anchor at Poughkeepsie and other river towns will carry him to the South Seas; the discovery of the Hudson will take him back to the Crusades; once one begins to follow the threads of local history, local manners, local industry, local peoples, one finds they lead in every direction.

Lewis Mumford, "The Value of Local History"

Chapter 1
PROLOGUE

*f*or thirteen thousand years, archaeologists tell us, Native Americans roamed the lands that now make up New York State. At least in more recent centuries, these peoples are known to have hunted, fished, grown corn and tobacco, and made their own tools. By a stream or near the edge of a forest, they built their villages of wigwams or of longhouses covered with bark.[1] The native peoples held sacred the lands and waters that fed them and named their tribes after them.

The Sepasco Tribe

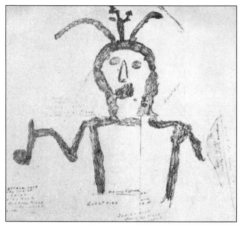

Rubbing made by Robert Bowne Suckley in 1930 of Native American petroglyph (circa 1100) found on a rock along the Hudson shore in southern Rhinebeck. Approximately 11 inches high. Dutchess County Historical Society Yearbook 1931.

The lands that now make up the Town of Rhinebeck, on the east bank of the Hudson River, halfway between Albany and New York City, once were stewarded by the Sepasco tribe. The name "Sepascot" came from the tribe's word for little river or stream (sepuus) and referred to the Landman's Kill, whose mouth (cot or coot) opens onto present-day Rhinebeck's southwestern shoreline. The natives cut a trail along that stream running east from the Hudson and built a settlement near what is now Lake Sepasco. The Sepascos belonged to the greater Lenape or Delaware tribe, along with the Esopus tribe, named for the Esopus Creek to the west of the Hudson.

Hendrick Hudson's Expedition

Having sailed the Atlantic on behalf of the Dutch West India Company on his ship *Half Moon* (Halve Maen), Hendrick Hudson put down anchor in October 1609 near Cruger's Island, offshore from present-day Red Hook. He was the first European known to sail so far up the Hudson, then called North River (Noort Rivier). On the way, his ship was visited almost daily by Native American bearing tobacco, beans, oysters, corn, and currants to trade with the sailors for knives, beads, and hatchets. This trading between the Dutch and native peoples continued for years in a mostly friendly fashion.

When Hendrick Hudson (inset) attempted to discover a passage to the Far East in 1609, his voyage led him to the river now bearing his name. His ship, The Half Moon, *has often been depicted in paintings and models. Henry Hudson from "The Hudson" by Benson J. Lossing. Half Moon from "The Hudson Fulton Celebration 1909," Vol 1, Albany J.B. Lyon Co, 1910.*

Early Dutch Settlements

In 1621, drawn more by the fur trade and other commercial interests than by the land, the Dutch claimed the New Amsterdam-Kingston-Albany area as their colony and called it New Netherlands. In 1664, the British, also attracted by the fur trade, took over of the colony. They met with no resistance from the Dutch, who were unwilling to risk the destruction of New Amsterdam and its businesses. Without shedding a

NEW AMSTERDAM, 1664.

New Amsterdam was clustered at the southern tip of Manhattan in 1664 when the British took it from the Dutch. From "The Hudson" by Lossing.

drop of blood, the British seized New Netherlands and renamed it New York. To secure their claim, they pushed to settle the colony with British subjects and encouraged petitions for land grants. These grants created self-contained farming networks like those of Europe's manorial system. At the center of each network was the landlord, who administered the surrounding leasehold and freehold farms. Although leaseholds were common in the colonies, their scale and extent in the Hudson Valley set the region apart and placed a peculiar stamp on its history.

Rhinebeck Indian Deeds and Patents

In the summer of 1686, three Dutch settlers from Kingston—Gerrit Artsen (of the family more commonly known as Van Wagenen), Arie Roosa, and Jan Elton (or Elting)—purchased land in Dutchess County from the Native Americans Aran Kee, Kreme Much, and Korra Kee. A few weeks later, a fourth Dutchman, Hendrick Kip, also from Kingston, bought land from the Native Americans Anamaton, Calycoon, and Ankony. The deeds of sale were both filed in Kingston. They detailed the transfer of a total of some 2,200 acres from the named Native Americans, described as members of the Sepascot and Esopus tribes, to

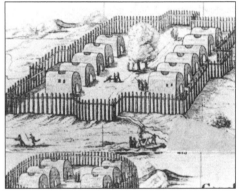

An Indian village of bark-covered dwellings drawn on a 1651 map of "Novi Belgii" (roughly the tri-state area) shows a log palisade enclosure. Experts believe that this sort of protection was used in times of unrest. New York State Library.

the four Dutch settlers, in exchange for "Six Buffaloes, Four Blankets, Five Kettles, Four Guns, Five Horns, Five Axes, Ten Kans of Powder, Eight Shirts, Eight Pairs of Stockings, Forty Fathoms of Wampum or Sewant, Two Drawing Knives, Two Adzes, Ten Knives, Half Anker Rum, One Frying Pan."[2]

Later in the summer of 1686, Hendrick Kip deeded some of his newly acquired parcel to his brother Jacob. In 1688, to secure their title to the land, the five Hollanders as partners applied for and were granted a royal patent, or land grant, by Thomas Dongan, Lieutenant Governor of New York Province. The patent recognized the new landholders and recorded the title. A small annual payment was usually required from the landholders. The parcels were settled by the Kip brothers and children of the other original patentees.

Kipsbergen

About 1700, near the old crossing at one end of the east-west Sepasco Trail in present-day Rhinecliff, the Kips established a community known as Kipsbergen. Hendrick Kip built his house in 1700 as shown by the lintel, now displayed in the Rhinebeck Post Office lobby. At first Kipsbergen consisted only of several houses, of which one served as meetinghouse. By 1717, however, the little settlement had become substantial enough to be made the official voting place for the North Ward of Dutchess County. For the short time it held the appointment, Kipsbergen served as the hub of local activities.

To the first settlers, as to those who came after them, the Hudson River was the heart of the region, providing landmarks, livelihood, the primary means of transporting people and goods, and beauty to nurture the soul. Peaceful and wide, banked by green hills and the gentle slopes of the Catskills, the river gave to the region a mood, a timelessness and tranquility. Washington Irving wrote about it: "[T]his glorious river... is... my first and last love ... [my] preference over all other rivers in the world. I seem to catch new life as I bathe in its ample billows and inhale the pure breezes of its hills."[3]

Lintel from the first known house in Rhinebeck is displayed in the post office lobby. Photo by Douglas Baz. *It is inscribed with the initials of the builder, Hendrick Kip (shown in inset) and his wife Annatje.*

This house, built circa 1708 by Jacob Kip, is the stone house located closest to the river on Long Dock Road. Museum of Rhinebeck History.

Ferry Service

Kip's ferry service is shown in this drawing. The ferry service operated between Kip's at Long Dock and Cantine's in Kingston. From "Historic Old Rhinebeck" by Howard H. Morse.

Isaac Kip, father of Hendrick and Jacob, sailed a sloop on the old river, trading and carrying freight between Albany, Kingston, and New York (then called New Amsterdam). In 1708, Jacob Kip launched a ferry service to Kingston from the Indian crossing at Kipsbergen, now called Long Dock, and built himself a stone house overlooking his dock and the river. Another Kip house was built in 1715, also of stone. Such stonework characterized Dutch building in the New World. Both houses still stand today as the oldest structures in town.

The custom in these early, sparse settlements was to designate one home as the local tavern, where weary travelers could sit down to a hot supper, hire a place to sleep for the night, exchange news and social pleasantries, and enjoy a drink or two. In Kipsbergen, that home was Abraham Kip's. Abraham, the son of Jacob Kip, obtained an exclusive charter to run the ferry as a commercial venturein 1752. Moses Cantine of Kingston was his partner. A ferry ran between Kingston and Rhinecliff until 1957, when the Kingston-Rhinecliff Bridge opened to traffic.

Settling Virgin Forests

It is hard to imagine today how unknown and untouched these lands were when the first Europeans came. The settlers mostly faced a dense wilderness of trees and ground vegetation, with a few footpaths and trails cut. But the natives had cleared some fields to grow their corn, and the soil was mostly loamy and promised good farming, and so the settlers kept coming. One Dutchman wrote:

The river offered Rhinebeck residents a rich assortment of fish such as sturgeon, bass and shad. New York State Watershed.

> *Our countryman... describe the wonderful size of the trees... Wild grapes are abundant, and walnut trees... [and] other trees, shrubs, and plants that grow spontaneously... The forests everywhere contain a great variety of wild animals... Innumerable birds are also found here... The rivers produce excellent fish, such as the salmon, sturgeon, and many others... I am therefore of the opinion that scarcely any part of America is better adapted for the settlement of colonies.*[4]

The King's Highway

In 1703, the Colonial Assembly of New York Province provided for the building of the Queen Anne's Highway, later named the King's Highway, a "Publick and Common General Highway... to extend... through the... County of Westchester, Dutchess County and the County of Albany, of the breadth of four rods." This road, later known as the Albany Post Road, became the main route for wagons, stagecoaches, and horses carrying people, supplies, and, most importantly, mail. To this day, as Route 9, it is the most used road in Dutchess County.

Albany Post Road's 100-mile marker, just north of Rhinebeck Village. Photo by Douglas Baz.

Self-sufficiency

Life in those times demanded a strong spirit. If a man wanted his land cleared, he took an axe to it himself. Farms were largely self-sufficient, supplying families with vegetables, fruits, game, veal, spring lamb, and dairy products. Churning butter, making cheese, putting up preserves, spinning wool and linen, weaving, sewing, and candlemaking all took place on the property. Couples produced large families, for they knew some of their offspring would not survive to adulthood. They also needed a large labor force. The father and his sons did the planting and harvesting, chopped the wood, cared for the animals, built the house and fences, and made the household utensils and furnishings. The mother and her daughters did the cooking and made the cloth, clothes, candles, and medicines. Small children fed the chickens, gathered eggs, and wove baskets. The whole family worked hard. Newly settled farmers quickly grew enough grain to sell their neighbors They also built mills so that they could sell flour to customers in New York City and the West Indies.

Dugout Dwellings

The construction of an early settler's homestead began with digging a room out of the side of a hill or bank. The "dugout" became the family shelter, providing protection from winter winds and summer heat. Later another room, and then a whole house, of wood, brick, or stone were built above the dugout. Even then it often continued to serve as the household kitchen and center of family life; at the start and end of the day everyone gathered around the hearth and its fire. The fire was always kept burning, even in summer. Cooking, spinning, sewing, weaving, eating, and sleeping—all the family's indoor life—took place in the dugout.

Abraham Kip house, built circa 1715, stands at the corner of Rhinecliff and Long Dock Roads. Museum of Rhinebeck History.

Such a room can be seen today in the old Abraham Kip house on Rhinecliff Road. A newspaper article appearing when his descendant, Rudolph Kip, owned the house, describes it this way:

The original kitchen of the first house… nestles against a protecting rise of ground on the west side, where the icy winds from the river cannot strike it. It was in rooms like this, protected from the elements, with very meager lighting, a huge fireplace for cooking, and for heating the room, that hundreds of families lived, and called it good… The fireplace was on the east wall of the room, the opposite west wall, snuggling into the protecting hill. Two small windows of three panes each were placed at ceiling height on the north and south walls. The ceiling was very low with 14-inch beams placed about forty inches apart. These are the largest timbers I have ever seen.[5]

The Beekman Patent

Another influential family staked its first claim in the area in 1697, when Judge Henry Beekman of Kingston received a royal patent for land "lying to the North of Hendrick Kip alongside the Hudson River, to the bounds of Major Peter Schuyler." A second patent, granted in 1703, more clearly defined the judge's holdings. It included all of the present Town of Rhinebeck except for the strip along the river, patented earlier to Kip-Artsen-Roosa-Elting.

Judge Henry Beekman (1652-1716). From "Historic Old Rhinebeck" by Howard H. Morse.

The Schuyler Patent, including what became the entire town of Red Hook, had been granted to Major—later Colonel—Peter Schuyler by King James II in 1688. Schuyler rapidly sold off many of these lands, including 5,541 acres to Judge Beekman's son, Colonel Henry, in 1715. The judge and his son were astute businessmen. They and their descendants dominated the economic and political life of Rhinebeck for many years. At the time, a young boy, gazing at the moon, is said to have remarked, "If there really is land on the moon, Mr. Beekman must own it." Judge Henry obtained land at the mouth of the Landsmanskill and established a mill and docks there about 1710.

Colonel Henry Beekman

With his vast property, Colonel Henry became landlord to much of Rhinebeck, leasing most of his land. He took possession of his father's mill in 1713, acquiring the central focus of the ecomomic activity in the town. Rye and wheat were the principal crops of his tenant farmers, and he required them to grind their grains exclusively at that mill. He collected his annual rents in bushels of wheat, "fat hens," or "days riding" (work done by the tenants for the mill or on the roads). With so much control over local economic life, the colonel was able to impose his will in local political life as well. He served as representative to the Provincial Congress for more than 40 years, between 1716 and 1758.

> *Mr. Filkin said he would provide or furnish Beef, Pork and bacon most all should be boiled a day or 2 before the Election and brought to the several houses of ours... Baltus Van Kleek bought 6 barrels of Cider... the cider should also be distributed before the day... I will send you my negro, Sam, till the Election be over... Bread we intend to bake here 100 loaves. Rum are to have from Bowdoin that also should be distributed.*

So wrote Henry Beekman to his nephew, Henry Livingston of Poughkeepsie on January 23, 1752, regarding customary election night festivities which were meant to reward the votes.

Kip-Beekman-Heermance House, built by Hendrick Kip, was sold to Col. Henry Beekman. For many years, it was known as the Beekman Manor House. The right-hand section was the prototype for the Rhinebeck Post Office. The house was destroyed by fire in 1908. Museum of Rhinebeck History. Inset: Colonel Henry Beekman, 1688-1776, lived in this house until his death. From "Historic Old Rhinebeck" by Howard H. Morse.

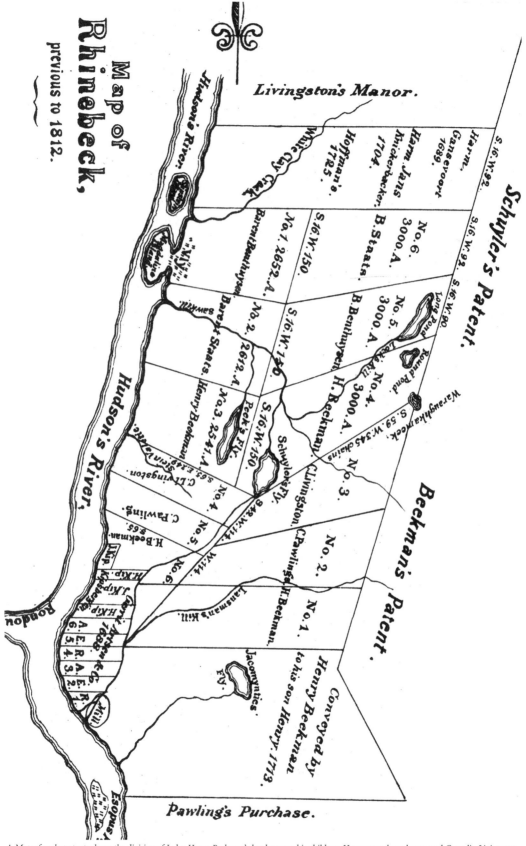

A Map of early patents shows the division of Judge Henry Beekman's land among his children. Henry was the only son and Cornelia Livingston (Mrs. Gilbert) and Catherine Rutsen Pawling (Mrs. Albert) were his daughters. From "History of Rhinebeck" by Smith.

Chapter 2
RHINEBECK SETTLEMENTS

*t*he Town of Rhinebeck, officially organized on March 7, 1788, evolved over time from several smaller settlements, including Kipsbergen described in *Chapter 1.* The first political division of Dutchess County in 1717 created North, Middle, and South wards. The present Red Hook and Rhinebeck were included in the North Ward. The Wards were further divided, and in 1738, Rhinebeck Precinct was established excluding the eastern portion of the North Ward.

The Palatines (Rhinebeck/Kirchoeck)

The first settlement to be called Rhinebeck grew up near the present-day intersection of Routes 9 and 9G. The area's first settlers were German immigrants from central Rhineland who were seeking a better life in the New World.

The German Palatines' lands had been plundered repeatedly by the French in the War of the Spanish Succession. Then the hard winter of 1708 and 1709 had killed many of their grapevines and other sources of food and livelihood. As vintners and farmers, they had endured unrelenting hardship in their native land; they could not resist the promises made by the British Crown. Intent on bringing settlers to its new territories, the British lured the Germans with a propaganda pamphlet know as "The Golden Book." The Palatines were promised plentiful harvests and ownership of the lands that produced them.

Of the original 13,000 Palatine immigrants to London, fewer than a quarter of them went on to New York, boarding 11 boats for the arduous crossing. Many of their number died en route from spoiled and inadequate provisions or rampant disease.

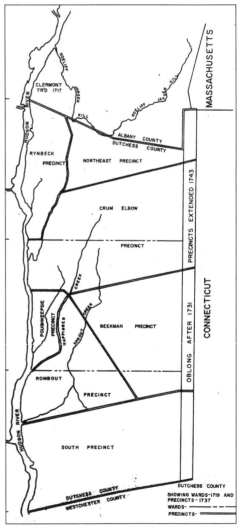

MacCracken map showing North, Middle, and South wards of Dutchess County and 1737 precinct division lines. From "Old Dutchess Forever" by MacCracken.

11

The Naval Stores Project

Finally, the Palantines landed in the summer of 1710, and undertook their obligation to repay the Crown for their passage. The immigrants had been assured that once their obligation was fulfilled, the British would provide each man with forty acres of land, free from quit rents and taxes for seven years.

Robert Hunter, governor of New York, arrived from London with the Palatines. His subsistence lists document the composition of individual Palatine families. From "Early Palatine Emigration" by Walter Knittle.

The Palatines first encamped at one of two sites: one on the far side of the Hudson, which is still called West Camp, and the other, then known as East Camp, now known as Germantown, in present day Columbia County. The latter was purchased for them from the 163,000-acres granted Robert Livingston by the Crown in 1686.

Between 1710 and 1712, they labored to extract tar for British ships from the native pines along the Hudson. Unfortunately, the project's management was ineffectual and corrupt, the Palatines lacked the necessary skills for the work, the trees were the wrong kind of pine, and finally, the British were unable to provide even the subsistence they had promised. With their dreams shattered, the Germans only barely survived the harsh winters.

Hearing of their plight from his friend Livingston, and eager to attract such industrious workers to his land, Judge Beekman offered them leaseholds on easy terms. While others of their original number either remained where they were or dispersed throughout the Schoharie and Mohawk valleys, 35 Palatine families accepted those terms and moved south. Henry Beekman's rent ledger shows some were already renting from him by late 1712.[6] These were the stalwart souls that began the community of Rhinebeck, named for the Rhine River (Rhyn) of their Palatine homeland and the Dutch word for brook (beck). (It is not known who decided on the name Rhynbeck, but it first appears in early Beekman correspondence of 1714.)

The First Church

In 1716, the Palatine settlers built a church where today Wey's Crossing Road meets Route 9 and only an ancient cemetery remains. The log structure was likely the first church constructed in Dutchess County. Reflecting these people's broad views, it served as the place of worship for both Lutheran and German Reformed congregations. It also was used as the community school—the first known school in the county—and as the site for informal mediation of disputes. Nearby, probably in a private home, town meetings were held and in 1737, the settlement took over from Kipsbergen as the precinct's voting center.

The Village at the Flatts

The settlement of what would become Rhinebeck Village began about 1706. Judge Beekman sold to William Traphagen a parcel of several hundred acres around the intersection of the east-west Sepasco Trail and the north-south King's

This log church, built in 1715 near Wey Road, was possibly the first church built in Dutchess County. Both the German Reformed and Lutheran congregations used it until 1730 when it was given to the German Reformeds. From "Historic Old Rhinebeck" by Howard H. Morse.

Footwarmer with pierced tin panels held coals to provide warmth in vehicles and at church service. Museum Of Rhinebeck History Collection. Photo by Douglas Baz.

"Rush lamp" used rush soaked in tallow or whale oil to provide a wick. Photo by Douglas Baz.

Highway (Route 9 today). Traphagen built his home on what is now West Market Street. It served as the village's first tavern and possibly as the site for public punishments; before it was demolished in 1868, the Traphagen house was to be known as "Old State Prison." The Dutchess County Supervisor's book shows that Abraham Freer was paid for making new stocks and iron work for the North Ward in 1731. Rudolf Kip received three pence for a lock for the stocks in 1732.[7]

The tavern now known as the Beekman Arms had a gambrel roof. It was a busy stage stop on the Albany Post Road. From "Historic Old Rhinebeck" by Howard H. Morse.

Traphagen sold off lots of his land to other Dutch proprietors, and soon a community, originally known as the Flatts, or Rhinebeck Flatts, took root at the intersection of the roads. There, facing King's Highway, Traphagen's son Arent is said to have built a tavern. The date associated with the building is 1766 so it was more likely built by Jacob J. Kip, after he married Arent's widow. Enlarged over the years, it still stands today as the Beekman Arms, named for Rhinebeck's most prominent family.

The Sepascot Tract

Another settlement took root when Colonel Henry Beekman granted leaseholds on a large parcel to Westfall and Company in 1719. This Sepascot Tract, named for the Native American tribe that had lived there, was a fertile stretch of land extending from present-day White School House Road to what became known as the Rock City community in the eastern part of town.[8] The leaseholders, Dutch families from Hurley in Ulster County, established themselves near present-day Patten Road on both sides of the stream there. In later years the area was known as Schooterhoek, meaning Shepherd's Corner.

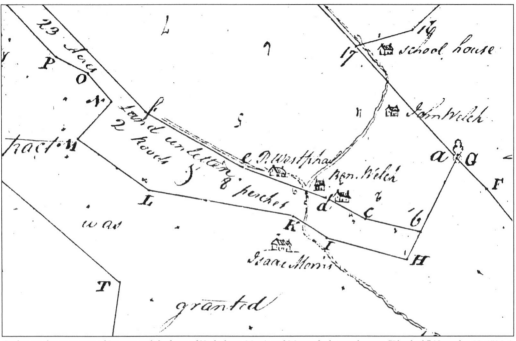

Settlement shown on map of Sepascot and the farms of Vredenburg, Morris and Weaver for lot number two, "Rhynbeck," November 25, 1786. A swampy, commons area was surveyed between the houses of Isaac Morris and Benjamin Welch on Patten Road. A portion of the Westphal house probably was built soon after 1719 when 513 acres were granted to Gilbert Westfall and company. New York State Library.

Detail showing exterior of Dutch door at Sepascot Farm. Divided doors served to keep children in the house and animals out, while providing light and air through the open top half. Photo by Nancy Kelly.

Interior of lower portion of Dutch door shows strap hinges and vertical boards typical of eighteenth century construction. Door was probably from the Vredenburg/Morris dwelling. Photo by Nancy Kelly.

14

Wurtemburg Tract

A second wave of German settlers arrived from Wuerttemberg, Germany, after 1730. They settled south and east of the village, in an area referred to on a map of 1802 as the "Wittemburgh tract."[9] Especially in the Wurtemburg area, the sturdy Dutch style barn was used. Some of the early barns built in the old Dutch style still stand today.

St. Paul's Lutheran Church, Wurtemburg. Built in 1802, on present-day Wurtemburg Road, east of Route 9G. Courtsey of Barbara Frost.

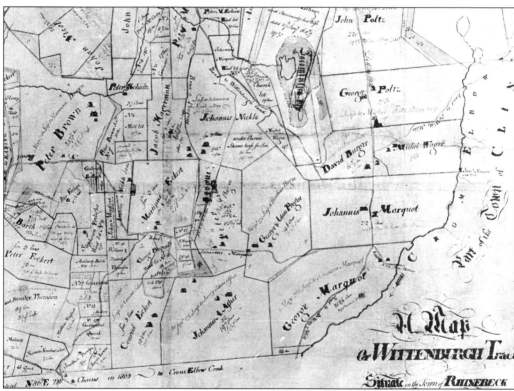

1802 map of the "Wittemburg Tract" shows the individual farms that made up the property of Morgan Lewis and his wife, Gertrude Livingston. Most of the southern portion of Rhinebeck was included. Names of the original settlers are noted on each parcel. Rhinebeck Historical Society.

The Dutch barn style was used on many Wurtemburg farms. It had a long sloping roof, bays for animals on each side and a threshing area with a hay mow in the center. The entrance was on the gable end. This barn was on the Marquart farm, on Wurtemburg Road near Schultz Hill Road. Quitman Resource Center National Register survey.

English-style barns featured entrances under the eaves and high sidewalls with steeper roofs than the Dutch style. Pictured here are the Losee barns adjacent to the old Rhinebeck cemetery. Photo by Marilyn Hatch.

Chapter 3
RHINEBECK GROWS

*I*n time Rhinebeck had sawmills to mill lumber for houses, barns, ships, and wagons, as well as mills for making grist, shingle, oil, and paper. Also, the storekeeper, wheelwright, cooper, harness maker, and, most important, the blacksmith had hung their shingles and were open for business.

Public Offices

This rock, prominent on the Rhinebeck shoreline south of the George Clinton Bridge to Kingson, marks the site of Schultz's or Mill's dock. Pearl Scism is pictured sitting on the rock. Museum of Rhinebeck History.

The titles held by public officers reflected the community's needs and concerns: "[A] Constable/Collector, two Assessors, an Overseer of the High Way, 2 Surveyors of the fences and a Pounder for offending Beasts" were cited in the 1718 Book of the Supervisors of Dutchess County. Having only barely emerged from the wilderness, the settlement needed to safeguard its lands from wildlife as well as from wandering domestic animals. Frequent payments were made, usually to Indians, for wolves' heads, for the animals posed a constant danger to the settlers.[10] In 1723, a regulation was passed requiring earmarks and brands to identify an owner's cattle, sheep, hogs, and horses, and setting the height of county fences at four feet.

Roads and Highways

Dr. George Miller, owner of the Schuyler house, stands near the site of the Rutsen Grist Mill on the Landsman Kill (circa 1900). Museum of Rhinebeck History.

Proper maintenance of the highway and roads was essential to the settlers' survival. A road master was appointed for each designated road district to ensure that property owners within the district fulfilled this responsibility. Until 1722, there was only one road in the North Ward; by 1749, there were ten road districts.[11] One of these districts included Pilgrim's Progress Road, which led from Rutsen's Mill on the Landsmans Kill, near the site of the Schuyler house, to the church on the Post Road and on to the river at Schultz's Landing. The Palatines depended particularly on this access to the river landing.

16

The Salisbury Turnpike

A law passed in April 1802 established a Turnpike Company to build a road from Salisbury, Connecticut through Rhinebeck to the Hudson River. The Rhinebeck-Salisbury Turnpike was built from Long Dock, through Rhinebeck, extending East Market Street from Center Street to the intersection with South Street, the former Sepascot Trail. The Turnpike followed the trail along the Landmans Kill, leaving the present 308 at Turnpike Road where it traveled East into Milan and on into Connecticut. The road substantially improved the transport of livestock and freight both

This bridge was built where the Salisbury Turnpike crossed the Landsman Kill near Miller Road. It was replaced in 2000 by a careful reproduction. Asher Collection.

eastward and westward through town, enhancing commerce and activity at Long Dock and bringing Rhinebeck into closer contact with New England. Local architect, Stephen Falatko, says that wonderful examples of Greek Revival Architecture found along East Market Street were a result of the turnpike and interaction with New England. Other Greek Revival structures, such as the Eighmeyville Schoolhouse and the Milan Methodist Church, are also found along the turnpike route.[12]

Detail from 1802 map for the Salisbury Turnpike shows the Sands house (burned 1999) at the bottom center. The Schuyler house is on the north of the Landsman Kill. Single dotted line shows the route of the Sepasco Trail, which preceded the Turnpike Road and followed the route of the present Schuyler Driveway. New York State Library.

Red Hook Formed

By 1812, the population of Rhinebeck had grown to such an extent that it was difficult to govern; on April 6, 1813, the town officially split into two towns, Rhinebeck and Red Hook. In 1817, the town clerk's office moved from the original Rhyn Beck settlement to the prospering village. Eventually, the part of town where the Palatines had settled came to be known as Pinks Corners, and the village, till then known as Rhinebeck Flatts, shortened its name to Rhinebeck. In 1834, the Village of Rhinebeck incorporated.

Moul's Inn is shown on the 1798 map of Rhinebeck. Rhinebeck town meetings were held here until 1817. Quitman Resource Center National Register survey.

Chapter 4
The Beekman Legacy

*n*ot even the eminent and well-to-do were immune from the severities of early colonial life. Colonel Henry Beekman, with such vast wealth to bequeath, had only one child—his daughter Margaret—who survived long enough to inherit it.

Margaret Beekman

Margaret Beekman (1724-1800), sometimes referred to as Rhinebeck's matriarch, was the only child to inherit Henry Beekman II's vast land-holdings. Reprinted by permission of Clermont State Historic Site, New York State Office of Parks, Recreation and Historic Preservation.

When Margaret Beekman, a formidable figure in her own right, married her cousin Judge Robert Livingston, grandson of the first lord of Livingston Manor, in 1742, the two most powerful families in the region were joined and a local dynasty was created. The couple's family was large—four sons and six daughters who lived to adulthood. Their sons and sons-in-law achieved national renown as leaders, public servants, business-men, and soldiers. Each in his own way would play a key role in formulating positions and planning strategies in the War of the Revolution and in forming our new country's civil government. In their time, the Beekman-Livingstons exerted considerable influence on the growth of the Town of Rhinebeck. The most visible evidence of their legacy was the estates they built overlooking the Hudson River, many of which still stand today.

The Chancellor

The most accomplished of the Livingstons' children was Chancellor Robert R. Livingston. He represented Dutchess County in the Provincial Congress that created New York State and at the First Continental Congress that drafted the Declaration of Independence. The State of New York appointed him its first chancellor (chief judge), and the new United States made him, prior to the establishment of a cabinet, its secretary of Foreign Affairs. As minister to France under the Jefferson Administration, he helped negotiate the Louisiana Purchase (1803). With his partner, inventor Robert Fulton, he launched the very first steamboat, *The Clermont*.

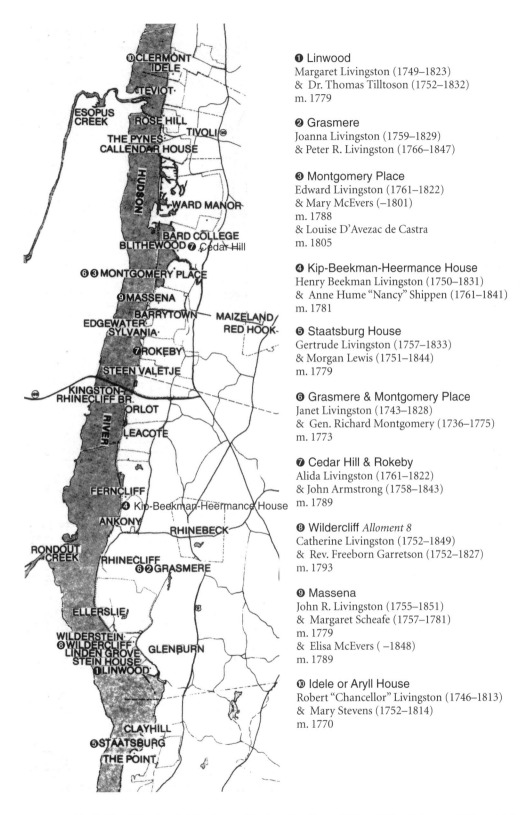

❶ Linwood
Margaret Livingston (1749–1823)
& Dr. Thomas Tilltoson (1752–1832)
m. 1779

❷ Grasmere
Joanna Livingston (1759–1829)
& Peter R. Livingston (1766–1847)

❸ Montgomery Place
Edward Livingston (1761–1822)
& Mary McEvers (–1801)
m. 1788
& Louise D'Avezac de Castra
m. 1805

❹ Kip-Beekman-Heermance House
Henry Beekman Livingston (1750–1831)
& Anne Hume "Nancy" Shippen (1761–1841)
m. 1781

❺ Staatsburg House
Gertrude Livingston (1757–1833)
& Morgan Lewis (1751–1844)
m. 1779

❻ Grasmere & Montgomery Place
Janet Livingston (1743–1828)
& Gen. Richard Montgomery (1736–1775)
m. 1773

❼ Cedar Hill & Rokeby
Alida Livingston (1761–1822)
& John Armstrong (1758–1843)
m. 1789

❽ Wildercliff *Alloment 8*
Catherine Livingston (1752–1849)
& Rev. Freeborn Garretson (1752–1827)
m. 1793

❾ Massena
John R. Livingston (1755–1851)
& Margaret Scheafe (1757–1781)
m. 1779
& Elisa McEvers (–1848)
m. 1789

❿ Idele or Aryll House
Robert "Chancellor" Livingston (1746–1813)
& Mary Stevens (1752–1814)
m. 1770

Map prepared by the Historic American Buildings Survey, 1973, shows River Estates. Children of Robert Livingston and Margaret Beekman, (grandchildren of Henry Beekman Jr.) are listed with their estates. Some estates correspond with the ten original allotments drawn by Margaret's children in 1787 by which the vast Beekman lands were divided.

Colonel Henry Beekman Livingston

Another of the Livingston's sons, Colonel Henry Beekman Livingston, organized the first infantry division in Dutchess County, the Fourth Regiment, under the command of his sister Janet's husband, General Richard Montgomery. He inherited the old Kip house from his Grandfather, Henry Beekman.

The Gentry Lifestyle

As country gentry, the Beekmans descendants led a different life from that of the Palatines and many of the other early Dutch settlers. Although the conditions of the times required simplicity even of the wealthy, the gentry lived well. Their income—in cash or in grain, hens, and labor—came primarily from canny administration of their lands, supplemented by profits from their mills, and sale or export of farm produce to New York City and beyond. For some, including the Livingstons, profits also came from a sideline in slave trade.[13]

Wealth was not evenly distributed in colonial Rhinebeck; the most prosperous ten percent of the community controlled 35 to 40 percent of its assets.[14] At first the social hierarchy was strictly two-tiered, with the Dutch preeminent and the Germans beneath them; over time the dividing line softened. Those confined by the lease hold system of land ownership found it more difficult to advance.

Particularly in the first half of the 18th century, women played an important role in commerce. Marriages were—had to be—equal partnerships. With workmen, indentured servants, and slaves to perform the manual labor, women not only ran their large households and oversaw the early secular and religious education of their children; they provided their husbands with political and commercial connections and engaged in overseas trade.[15] Dutch law gave women and men equal economic rights, and this spirit of equality was maintained in New York Province until the British conquest of 1664. From then on, the settlers were subject to British common law, which deprived married women of a legal identity and prevented them from owning property and signing contracts. Female entrepreneurs continued their commerce, but from behind their husbands' signatures. Later, after families established a large network of members in the area business began to be delegated solely to men, and the role of women changed. The ladies were trained and educated more as their husbands' ornaments and social diplomats than as partners in enterprise. While the women took care of the households, the men gave the bulk of their time to public service as local officials or representatives in the legislature. They also spent time entertaining other local worthies and British governors.

Often the gentry kept houses in New York City for the harsh winter months. They would travel the river by sloop or on the Albany-New York Post Road by stage.

Chapter 5
SLAVERY

throughout the 18th century, Rhinebeck's rich and not-so rich settlers owned slaves. Slavery was an accepted institution, in the North and in the South, although Northern farmers needed fewer hands to work their grain fields than were needed to work the Southern plantations. Most families in the area kept only one or two slaves, while the wealthier often had 10 or more.[16] With fewer numbers to manage, Northern slave-owners kept fewer records about their human property than did their Southern counterparts, and so we know less about the Northern slaves' daily life.

Receipt of sale of "one certain Negro man named Lewis" to John Teller by Andries P. Heermance, March 30, 1796. Rhinebeck Town Historian, Teller Collection.

Living Conditions

It seems slaves, were used as farm laborers and domestic servants, and to perform other unskilled labor. Indentured servants, workmen, and leaseholders performed tasks requiring greater skills. The slaves were housed in their owner's cellar, attic, or outbuildings, or boarded with tenants. Although it was in the owner's interest to keep them clothed, fed, healthy, and not too discontent, they had no legal rights to such care. Slaves were seated separately in the balconies of churches and buried in a separate section of the Rhinebeck Cemetery. More often than not, the members of slave families were separated from their kinfolk and sold to different, often distant, households.

The balcony on three sides of the interior of the Dutch Reformed Church in Rhinebeck provided seating for "colored" members of the congregation. Photo by Douglas Baz.

Traders brought the slaves over by ship from Africa and the West Indies to New York to be sold or traded like chattel. Slaves bound upstate were taken by sloop up the Hudson to their new owner's home or else to change hands once again. In a bill of sale dated 1790, "Gappy Van Vradenburgh of the Town of Rhinebeck,... Widow" sold "a Negro Girl valued at the sum of Seventy five pounds" to George Shumaker,... farmer."[17] The census of 1755 recorded 52 slaveholders and 116 slaves in Rhinebeck precinct;[18] by 1790, there were 421 slaves.[19] (Despite the Livingstons' key role in Rhinebeck history, their slaves were not included in the 1755 total, as *Clermont*, the family residence, was just over the border in Columbia County.)

Until just after the Revolution, there was a shortage of labor in the New York colony that supported the practice of slavery. After 1763, however, white immigration increased and there seemed less need for the expense involved in the upkeep of slaves. By the 1780s, a number of prominent New York citizens, motivated by economic advantage as well as ideals, had launched a campaign to set the slaves free.

Reverend Freeborn Garrettson

Reverend Freeborn Garrettson, a leading Methodist, Rhinebeck resident, and husband of Chancellor Livingston's sister, Catherine, was a strong abolitionist. Others holding comparable political and economic sway fiercely defended their right to slave property. The slaves themselves were not passive in their emancipation, but fought for it as they could by purchasing their liberty, joining the Continental Army, absconding with loved ones, writing petitions demanding freedom, and gaining concessions from their owners to maintain the integrity of their families.

Freeborn Garrettson (1752-1827) was an influential in establishing Methodism in the northeastern United States.

Reverend Frederick H. Quitman

Desk of Reverend Fredrick Quitman is displayed in the front parlor at the 1798 Quitman house. His silhouette is shown placed on the desk's writing surface. Photo by Douglas Baz.

A law was passed in 1785 that encouraged manumission, and an Act of Legislature was passed on April 8, 1801, that allowed for the manumission of those slaves able to provide for themselves. The Reverend Frederick H. Quitman, pastor at St. Peter's Lutheran (Stone Church) was the first Rhinebeck resident recorded in the town's Record of Manumission of Slaves.[20] He set free a woman named Eme and her child, Jack. (On the other hand, the Reverend's son, General John A., who spent much of his adult life in Mississippi, was one of the South's most ardent defenders of slavery.)

But not until 1817 did unconditional emancipation of all slaves over 28 years of age as of July 4, 1827, become law in the New York State Legislature. However by then the slaves were dependent on their owners, so freedom was not always the kindest option. In this rural setting and its less than friendly society, it was difficult for the newly freed to establish communities to assure themselves of economic and spiritual support. In her will, Margaret Beekman, concerned for those who had provided her with such "faithful services," granted manumission to her slaves over age 30 provided they "may desire it." Knowing that some were "far advanced in life and unable to support themselves by their Labour," she gave them the choice of living with her children.[21] Many freed slaves stayed on with the families of their original owners as paid laborers.

Reverend Robert Scott

In the 1830s, the Underground Railway began its clandestine transporting of slaves up from the South, through the Northern states, to freedom in Canada. Local lore has it that the people of Rhinebeck were committed enough to emancipation that they dug a number of secret passageways and tunnels, carving out a route from the Hudson River to Connecticut in service to the cause. The Baptist Church, founded by Reverend Robert Scott, is thought to have been especially active in the Underground Railroad.

The First Baptist Church, now the northern part of a restaurant on Montgomery Street. Rhinebeck Historical Society.

The Last of the Indians

Various records refer to the presence of the Indians in the Rhinebeck area through the 1800s. Volume VII of Documents Relating to the Colonial History of New York, for example, cites the shooting of a young Indian man by a white man near "Reinbeck" around 1748. The incident led to mediation between Indians and whites that resulted in an agreement. Generally, settlers were cautious of the natives but did their best to maintain smooth relations.

Arrowheads collected on the Ferncliff estate span a succession of time periods in archeological history. Museum of Rhinebeck History. Photo by Douglas Baz.

Meanwhile, the buying up of Indian lands by white settlers continued. With no more land to sell and little of value to trade, the Native Americans, with only a few exceptions, were either exterminated or driven north. Little knowledge of their history and way of life has been saved, for the habits, customs, and costumes of the natives were looked upon as too absurd and savage to preserve a record of them. The result is that we probably know less of these Indians today than of any on the American continent.[22]

The last Sepasco Indian is said to have died in 1867 in a hut near Welch's Cave and Lake Sepasco.

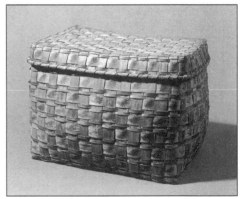

Native American basket imprinted with leaf and geometric designs. This type of basket was woven for trade by Native Americans remaining in the area. Descendents of the Sepasco tribe probably wove it. Photo by Douglas Baz.

Before the Revolution

As the settlers made themselves more at home in the new land, the quality of their lives improved from bare subsistence, to managing well, to even producing a surplus. In time they had goods to offer—flax seed, rum, grain, elk and deer skins, ox horns, lumber, beeswax, tobacco, blubber and hops. These were traded for silks, china, and other luxury items from England and other countries of Europe, as well as for staples like sugar and molasses from the West Indies. The British levied taxes on goods imported from non-British sources that the settlers eventually found intolerable. When they appealed in a friendly way for revision, the Crown mobilized its soldiers on American turf to collect payment, with force if necessary. In 1775, the colonists protested with the Boston Tea Party and resisted in clashes on the fields at Concord and Lexington.

Tenant Unrest

Related to the New York colonists' problems with the British, was the split within their own province between landowner and tenant. This split was virtually feudal in its effect: Those owning the land had all the wealth and power, while the leaseholders clearing and farming that land had only debts and taxes to pay. When the British insisted upon their taxes, the farmers not only protested, they also demanded title to the lands they had worked for so long, as well as representation in the British Parliament.

RECEIVED this _forthen_ Day of March 1766 from _Mattys Brogh_ of _Rhinebeck_ Precinct _fiften Shepples_ of merchantable Winter Wheat, _one days ryting_ _two fouls_ on Account of _farm rent_ for and in Behalf of _Colo Henry Beekman Esqr_ _by me Henry Dencker_

1766 Rent Receipt shows that Rent of 15 scheples wheat, one days riding and two fowl, paid by Matthias (Mattys Brogh) Progue was accepted by the miller, Henry Dencker for Henry Beekman. Matthias kept receipts from the years 1747–1785 which were bound together and discovered at a church in Michigan where his descendants had probably moved. Museum of Rhinebeck History.

A Palatine who settled on Ackert Hook Road, near Wurtemburg, Matthias Progue (Brogh) 1709–1795, lived on land shown west of the church on the Lewis Map. His stone house was built about 1762. Quitman Resource Center National Register Survey.

Chapter 6
THE AMERICAN REVOLUTION (1775–1783)

by spring 1775, the colonists supporting a break with England had become a majority, if not an eager one. It also was determined that the Articles of Association, also known as The Pledge, would be circulated for signature among the people of New York Province. In Rhinebeck, Egbert Benson was put in charge of securing support for this resolution, dated April 29, 1775:

> *To adopt and endeavour to carry into execution whatever measures may be recommended by the Continental Congress or resolved upon by this Provincial Congress for the purpose of preserving our Constitution, and opposing the execution of the several arbitrary and oppressive acts of the British Parliament, until a reconciliation between Great-Britain and America, on constitutional principles... can be obtained.*

The Signers

Two hundred twenty-nine residents of Rhinebeck Precinct, including Philip G. Livingston and Colonel Henry Beekman, signed the pledge protesting taxation without representation; 218 would not sign and so were listed as Tories and relieved of the firearms in their possession.[23]

The Bogardus Tavern, now the Beekman Arms, was the scene of militia drills. In this photograph, Dutch Arms Drum and Fife Corps re-enact the drills at the time of the Bicentennial in 1976. Museum of Rhinebeck History.

The first meeting of the Continental Congress was called that May. New York was asked to raise an army of 10,000 in preparation for war against the British Crown. The First Provincial Congress of New York met later that month, setting a course for recruiting the quota of troops.

By June 1775, Dutchess County had recruited enough men from its tenant farmers and freeholders to fulfill its quota and make up four divisions. One of these was led by Henry Beekman Livingston. His company drilled on the lawn of the Bogardus Tavern (Beekman Arms), the establishment once operated by Arent Traphagen.

General Washington Visits

In August, the newly appointed general of the Continental Army, George Washington, came to Dutchess County to study the area's defenses, anticipating the tactical importance in the war of the Hudson River region.

General Montgomery Killed

In September, Dutchess County recruits marched north with Brigadier-General Richard Montgomery. Husband of Janet Livingston and a former soldier of the king, now second-in-command under Major-General Philip Schuyler, Montgomery had not assumed his appointment readily, but had to be convinced by General Washington to leave his wife of less than two years. General Montgomery and his troops moved through Albany and then farther north toward Quebec to secure possession of the British strongholds to the north. Although suffering heavy losses, Montgomery succeeded in capturing St. John and Montreal, giving the Americans their first gains on the British. From there he moved on to Quebec, leading his own handful of men and a small number of reinforcements that had joined him under Colonel Benedict Arnold. It was in the course of the attack on Quebec that Montgomery became the first American general to fall in battle, shot through the head on December 31, 1775. With the loss of their leader, his troops were forced to withdraw in defeat.

The chapter house of the Daughters of the American Revolution was the home of Janet and Richard Montgomery at the time of the Revolution. The house was moved from Montgomery Street to 66 Livingston Street in 1860. Quitman Resource Center National Register Survey.

"Death of Montgomery Before Quebec," engraving after a painting by John Trumbull. General Montgomery became a national hero with towns and counties named in his honor throughout the United States. Nancy Kelly Collection.

Janet Montgomery

This house on Mill Road called Grasmere was being built for Janet and Richard Montgomery when he left for the war. Later, Grasmere was acquired by Janet's brother-in law, Peter R. Livingson, and his wife Joanna. It was rebuilt after an 1828 fire. Quitman Resource Center National Register Survey.

General Montgomery's death was felt keenly by his countrymen—he became a national hero—and by his devoted wife. Janet Montgomery planted flowering locust trees in memory of her husband and his men. The descendants of these trees still stand today, straight as soldiers, along Rhinebeck's Mill Road and the road to the Montgomery mansion, now known as *Grasmere.* Thirty years after the General's death, Janet built *Montgomery Place* near the river in Red Hook where she lived for the rest of her life. *Grasmere* was rented to Morgan Lewis until he built another home in Staatsburgh. At that point, the property was sold to Janet's brother-in-law, Peter R. Livingston, whose home had been on West Market Street in the village.

General Montgomery had written to his wife on December 10, 1775:

I begin to admire much your Heroism—you have more of it at present than I am possessed of. I wish most sincerely to sit by my own fireside—let others by their military talents seek for applause... Nothing but a very gloomy prospect indeed that draws me out of my nest.[24]

The Declaration of Independence

During the spring of 1776, the Declaration of Independence of the United States of America was drafted with the help of Rhinebeck's leading citizen, Robert R. Livingston.[25]

Military Action

Much of the Revolution's military action was concentrated in the Province of New York in 1777. The British laid siege to New York City and Westchester County and began to move north. As General Washington had foreseen, they planned to gain control of the Hudson River, there by dividing New York and isolating New England from the Southern colonies. Washington ordered that a great iron chain be stretched across the river to block the enemy navy's progress, but the 1,800 feet and 50 tons of links were broken apart by the tides. The British, in 30 to 40 ships commanded by General Vaughn, sailed through and northward as fast as they could.

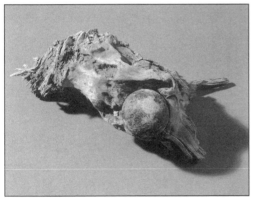

Cannon ball embedded in a tree root found nearly a mile from the Hudson River off Fox Hollow Road. This seems to provide evidence of the 1777 British shelling of Rhinebeck from the river. Museum of Rhinebeck History Collection. Photo by Douglas Baz.

Iron chain link believed to be from the chain used at West Point. Museum of Rhinebeck History Collection. Photo by Douglas Baz.

The Burning of Kingston

On October 16, the British launched a cannon barrage against Kingston, then the capitol of the province. The attack was sighted across the river by a Rhinebeck militia officer, Barent Van Wagenen, who then rode hard to the Village of Rhinebeck and Wurtemberg to warn the citizenry and rally the militia. The following day, Van Wagenen sighted a British boat landing at Long Dock. This news, too, he spread on behalf of his countrymen. But the enemy, proceeding on foot up River Road were still able to damage homes and blast a cannon hole in Colonel Beekman's gable. The log of the British ship *Dependence,* shows that the British fleet rested near Cruger's Island before continuing further north and setting more fires—most notably to Margaret Livingston's *Clermont* and to all the Livingston mills.[26]

General Putnam's Pursuit

Meanwhile, the Americans' General Israel Putnam and his troops followed on land the British fleet's movements upriver. When the British finally learned of Putnam's pursuit and of their General Burgoyne's surrender at Saratoga (October 7, 1777), they turned back to their ships and began a retreat.

General Israel Putnam commanded American troops as they followed the movements of the British ships upstream. Many local militiamen were under his command. From "Pictorial Field Book of the Revolution" by Benson J. Lossing.

The fighting at Saratoga is depicted in this etching. T.F. Donnelly. From "A Primary History of the United States" (1885) Rhinebeck Town Historian.

Articles of Confederation

Earlier in 1777, Kingston had hosted the convention that drafted the Constitution of New York State. However, after Kingston's charring in 1778, the capitol of New York was moved from there to Poughkeepsie. The first act of the New York State Senate was to ratify the Articles of Confederation, the nation's first set of laws, in February of that year.

The Economics of War

The war brought shortages, inflation, a flood of worthless currencies, and a blockade of New York City that halted all imports. Fired by necessity and faith, the Dutchess County colonists turned the economic hardships of war into gains. They developed an intricate local network that linked trade and agriculture, services and products; that encouraged neighborliness and cooperation and discouraged self-interest at the expense of the community as a whole. They instituted price controls, both formally through legislation, and informally through group pressure. While the men were off fighting or tending to policy, the women organized boycotts against British goods, stepped up home production of clothing and other things once imported, and led crowd actions against price-gouging merchants. At one store: "the women! In this place have risen in a mob, and are now selling a box of tea of yours [the owner] at 6s per lb."[27]

More goods were produced; plus, more were sold or exchanged on the market than were kept for the household. Bartening decreased and the use of paper currency increased. The market grew. With the Continental Army encamped at nearby Fishkill, the demand for produce was steady and strong. New York became one of the leading wheat-growing states in the new nation, and the fertile fields of the mid-Hudson Valley were its wheat-growing stronghold, the "breadbasket" of the Revolution. Beef, textiles, lumber, slate, flax, and other grains were shipped from this region as well.

Burgoyne's Surrender

From Burgoyne's surrender through war's end, with the signing of the Treaty of Paris in 1783, no more fighting took place in Dutchess County, though the people of Rhinebeck continued to give supplies and men to support the American cause.

Federalism

Individuals from Rhinebeck, Kingston and Poughkeepsie, all played key roles in the ratification of our national Constitution. Beginning in 1787, the process preceding the document's acceptance involved a long, heated, and complex debate over the rights of the national government versus those of the individual states.

In Dutchess County, the debate between Federalists, who believed in a centralized nation government and anti-Federalists, who believed the states should have more power, was inseparable from the longstanding conflicts between landlord and tenant. The hostility of the anti-Federalists toward the Federalists was also that of the leaseholders toward the landowning aristocracy. The anti-Federalists professed that the Federalists could not "have that sympathy with their constituents which is necessary to connect them closely with their interests."[28]

Constitution Debate

On June 17, 1788, a convention was called at the courthouse in Poughkeepsie to consider how New York State should vote on the proposed Constitution. Governor George Clinton chaired the debates. Interest in the proceedings was high; contrary to custom, women came out with the men to witness them. Prior to the debates, New Yorkers Alexander Hamilton and John Jay and Virginian James Madison had launched a unique campaign for ratification: they had published a

Unusual handmade 13-star flag, circa 1778. Museum of Rhinebeck History. Photo by Frank L. Asher.

series of commentaries over a period of six months in four New York City newspapers. The 85 essays are now known as *The Federalist Papers*. Far more considered than mere propaganda, the essays offer a deeply searching discussion of the Constitution.

Chancellor's Role at the Convention

Chancellor Robert R. Livingston, from Rhinebeck, played a strategic role at the convention.

Working closely with Hamilton and Jay, he negotiated successfully with wavering delegates behind the scenes. However, his speeches to the convention, which were generally marked by a haughty, aristocratic tone, were not very effective in bringing over avowedly anti-Federalist delegates elected by ordinary farmers and workers.[28]

Ratification

When the State of Virginia voted in favor of the Constitution assuring ratification, New York acceded as well. It was the eleventh of the thirteen states to do so.[29]

Chancellor Robert Livingston shown with Jefferson and Franklin; the committee to draft the Declaration of Independence. Rhinebeck Town Historian.

Washington Sworn into Office

When George Washington was voted the first president, he was sworn into office by Chancellor Livingston, the chief justice of New York.

Slow Demise of Leaseholds

Not until after 1846 did a constitutional amendment ease the leasehold system in New York State. To this day in the village of Rhinebeck, those owning homes on church land pay an annual quit rent of about $10 to the Dutch Reformed Church, in keeping with a stipulation by Henry Beekman from more than two centuries ago.[30]

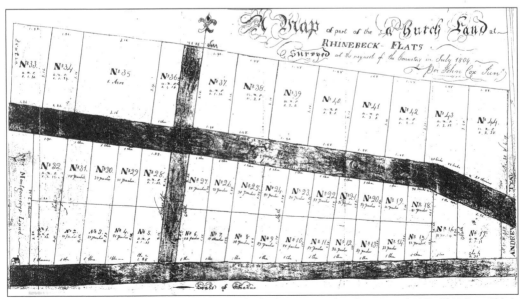

Map of part of the Church Land at Rhinebeck Flats, 1804 A rent list dated Oct 16, 1799, shows Lots 1,2,5,14 & 19 Daniel McCarty, 3 Maria Churchil, 4 Martin Heermance, 6 ,7&42 Henry Norris, 8 Jacob Schultz, 9 Wm P. Hoghteeling, 10 & 11 William Radclift, 12&21 Jacob Hendricks, 13&20 Gerrit VanWagenen, 15&18 Aristides Tompkins, 16 Peter Snyder, 17&30 Adam Shufelt, 22 Tobias P. Stoutenburgh, 23 Richard Bucktree, 24 Jacob Rider, 25 Samuel Lyons, 26 Abraham Vanderhoof, 27 George Cox, 28,36&37 Aaron Camp, 29 Frederick Tator, 31 Henry Teal, 32 Caleb Rider, 34&33 James Dunham, 38 Jacob Schultz, 39 Ephraim Herrick, 40 James Simpson, 41 John Teller. Reformed Dutch Church, Rhinebeck.

Chapter 7
PROSPERITY AND THE RIVER PLACES

*a*lthough New York's leaseholds and manorial system kept some settlers away, the state's population doubled between 1760 and 1781. After the Revolution, a new prosperity came to Rhinebeck and Dutchess County.

The economic good fortune fostered a new breed of gentry who, as essayist Nathaniel Parker Willis observed, "could afford to let the trees grow." The first of these were Margaret Beekman's ten children. They had been assigned their lands from their grandfather's vast estate according to their mother's instructions: by drawing straws. There were also the estates built by the descendants of Colonel Henry Beekman's sisters, and others of Rhinebeck's long-prominent families: Livingstons, Rutsens, Sands, Suckleys, and Schuylers. These families could support city and country households and were no longer dependent upon farming for a livelihood. They could afford to invest in parcels with less fertile land and more extravagant views looking out on the Hudson and Catskills.

Retreating from the fray of city life, "the river families," as they came to be known, created of their country estates small private worlds. They dedicated themselves to studies in animal husbandry, agriculture, and horticulture, to forming agricultural societies, and to publishing farming journals. They also experimented with many styles of art, architecture, and landscape design, often competitive with each other for the most avant-garde and high-style. In the process, they built homes that became paradigms of every architectural style, from federal to modern.

Wildercliff

One such home and estate was *Wildercliff*. This was the home of Catherine Livingston Garrettson and her husband, the Reverend Freeborn Garrettson, who preached the first Methodist sermon in Rhinebeck in 1788 and later achieved renown as a pacifist and abolitionist. The couple's riverfront home had been built on land acquired through a trade with Johannes Van Wagenen who settled on the Garrettson's property east of the Schuyler House.

VIEW FROM WILDERCLIFF.

"View from Wildercliff," *etching from B. Lossing, 1866, shows an expansive view down the river.* From "The Hudson" by Lossing.

Linwood

Another one of these grand homes was *Linwood,* owned by Margaret Livingston Tillotson and her husband Thomas Tillotson, who was surgeon-general during the Revolution. Pete Johnson, whose father had been a slave at *Linwood,* passed on the story of his father's meeting General Washington there sometime around 1796:

> *The Gen'l, he rode on a white hoss, with green an' gold trimmin's. He wore a big yaller hat. He used to take off dat hat to a cullud pussun same as to a white pusson. Lawsy, 't made no difference to him.*[31]

A century later, Henry James wrote about *Linwood*—his visits there as a boy left a lifelong mark upon him.

Thomas Tillotson (1752-1832) was surgeon general for George Washington. After Tillotson married Margaret Livingston, he bought the property surrounding Beekman's Mills at the mouth of the Landmanskill. Museum of Rhinebeck History.

George Washington gave as a wedding gift to the Tillotsons a set of tables that could be combined to provide a dining table. Olin Dows proudly displayed them at Glenburn and willed them to Clermont State historic site where they are currently in storage. Asher Collection.

Staatsburgh House

General Morgan Lewis (1754-1844) married Gertrude Livingston, May 11, 1779. From "Historic Old Rhinebeck" by Howard H. Morse.

The house which formerly stood on the site of the Mills mansion in Staatsburg belonged to Gertrude Livingston and her husband General Morgan Lewis. Lewis had distinguished himself as a leader of the Continental army. He was appointed attorney general of New York State in 1791, and served as the state's chief justice from 1801 to 1804, when he was elected governor. He acquired a large portion of Henry Beekman's land in southern Rhinebeck. In 1802 his landholdings in Rhinebeck extended from the Artsen-Roosa patent along the river to the eastern and southern town lines.[32]

Rokeby

Rokeby, at Barrytown, was home to John Armstrong, husband of Alida Livingston. He was first a general, then U.S. senator, minister to France, and secretary of war during the War of 1812.

Schuyler House

Sally Rutsen, a direct descendent of Judge Henry Beekman, married Philip Jeremiah Schuyler, son of the revolutionary general, and they built an estate near the falls of Landmans Kill. Schuyler's sister was married to Alexander Hamilton. That's why he received an express letter, dated July 11, 1804, reporting the outcome of the duel fought between Hamilton and Aaron Burr:

General Hamilton has this morning been dangerously wounded by Burr. The ball entered his side and it is feared has injured the spinal marrow.[33]

John Armstrong (1758-1843) married Alida, youngest daughter of Margaret Beekman and Robert Livingston. Their home, Rokeby, is located in Red Hook. From "The Empire State" by Lossing.

Philip Jeremiah Schuyler (son of Philip Schuyler, the Revolutionary War general) married Sally Rutsen, a descendant of the first Henry Beekman. Rhinebeck Historical Society.

This photograph, circa 1865, shows the Schuyler house. It was probably taken from the Salisbury Turnpike route, which passed between the house and the barns. Rokeby Collection.

Chapter 8
ROMANTICISM

*t*he estates of the Livingston children, along with the other river places lining the east bank of the Hudson, helped root Romanticism in the New World. Originating in England, and an influence here roughly between 1790 and 1865, the Romantic Movement affirmed the value of the individual, of emotion over rationalism, of nature over cities, of the spiritual over the material—of "sublime thoughts" over "penny wisdom," as Ralph Waldo Emerson extolled it.

Art and Architecture

Detailed of 1850 map of Dutchess County shows landowners and locations of residents. Museum of Rhinebeck History.

The Romantic movement in America was imbued with the spirit of the Revolution, and a reaction to the Puritan ethic, the conquest of the wilderness, and the growth of wealth and commerce. The Hudson River and its surrounding mountains and hills, just as nature had made them, embodied American Romanticism to the artists and writers of the day. From love of the river and its surroundings, the Hudson River School of painting evolved, as did a literature and a style of architecture and landscape design that reached its highest expression in the River Places. Many of the river estates that had been built in earlier times were added to, renovated, or rebuilt in the romantic spirit. Alexander Jackson Davis, Richard Upjohn,

The Delamater house, (above) designed by A. J. Davis, was constructed in 1844 for Henry Delamater, president of the First National Bank of Rhinebeck. Museum of Rhinebeck History. *Henry Delamater, (left) shown with his dog, was one of many wealthy and prominent residents of the village during the nineteenth century.* DAR.

George Veitch, Stanford White, and Richard Hunt were architects who enhanced their national reputations with their designs for Rhinebeck mansions. Landscape artists Calvert Vaux and Louis Ehlers, and the influence of Andrew Downing, helped reshape the lands and gardens of the great houses.

Edith Wharton

A romantic landscape design was naturalistic, made of contoured green spaces planted with a variety of trees and ground vegetation—some native, some exotic—arranged not by formal scheme, but to follow the lay of the land. In the revolt against classical restraint, these landscapes evoked mood and emotion—which at their extreme could become gothic. Influenced by her girlhood visits to an aunt's home in Rhinecliff, Edith Wharton, in *The Age of Innocence,* describes such a gothic place:

Wyndcliffe, a Norman-style mansion, built by Edith Wharton's aunt, Elizabeth Jones, is now a ruin. In its day, it was greatly admired. Museum of Rhinebeck History.

> *From the high ground on which it stood a series of terraces... descended... to a small irregular lake with an asphalt edge overhung by rare weeping conifers. To the right and left, the famous weedless lawns studded with "specimen" trees... rolled away to long ranges of grass...*

> *Against the uniform sheet of snow and the greyish winter sky the Italian villa loomed up rather grimly; even in summer it kept its distance, and the boldest coleus bed had never ventured nearer than thirty feet from its awful front.*

National Landmark District

In 1990, the secretary of the Interior designated the strip of country seats running from Columbia County, north of Clermont down to Staatsburg, south of Rhinebeck, as the Hudson River National Historic Landmark District, perhaps the largest of its kind in the nation. The criteria for the designation are three: "1. the district is nationally significant for its association with events that... represent the... patterns of United States history; 2. the district illus-trate(s) a significant aspect of our national

The Hudson River Historic District follows the river for sixteen miles from Columbia County to Staatsburg. It was designated in 1990. Photo by Douglas Baz.

culture; and 3. the district represents a great ideal of the American people... American Romanticism is an aspect of its history that transcends an event... Romanticism is one of the (mid-Hudson Valley's) most significant contributions to the nation, and its manifestation on the landscape is one of the nation's treasures."[34]

Chapter 9
RIVER TRANSPORTATION

a strong trade network needs a strong transportation system; for this, the people of Dutchess County had always relied on the Hudson River. Through the start of the 19th century, sloops and the ferry services launched from Kip's, and then other docks, continued to run people, horses, produce, dry goods, timber, and slate up to Albany, down to New York City, and across to Kingston. River travel was in for its own revolution, however. It came with Robert Fulton's invention of the steamboat. Named the *Clermont,* the steamboat's first trip up the Hudson in 1807

The ferry dock as it appeared about 1945. Asher Collection.

The ferryboat Transport was divided; half for pedestrians and vehicles and the other for animals destined for Kingston slaughterhouses. In 1897 passage cost 13 cents. The ferry made 26 trips per day. Asher Collection.

The day liner, the Mary Powell was one of the most beautiful of the riverboats. It followed a regular schedule between New York and Albany. From the "Hudson River Day Liner" by Donald C. Ringwald.

amazed its observers. In 1811, one witness described it thus: "a boat moving without appearance of sail, oar, pole, or any manual labor—moving within the secrets of her own mechanism and propelled by power undiscoverable."[35] The speed and power of steamboats meant new possibilities—of trade in more perishable goods, of travel in less favorable tides and winds, and later, particularly on the Hudson, of a pleasure cruise with friends on a boat like the elegant *Mary Powell.*

Influences of "Clinton's Ditch"

The next great advancement in transportation—the Erie Canal—opened in 1825. This manmade waterway linked the Atlantic Ocean to Lake Erie, by way of New York Harbor, the Hudson, and Albany. The canal made it possible to travel west of the Appalachians without confronting either the mountains or the Mohawk River's rapids and waterfalls. The Erie paid for itself with the tolls collected in its first seven years of operation. Its success ushered in the Canal Age and transformed the way of life in New York and in the nation. As had been anticipated, the canal opened up westward travel. It also attracted immigrants and other settlers to the frontier; cut shipping costs; made New York Harbor the country's greatest port; encouraged the building of a complete water route from New York City to New Orleans. It caused a gradual decline in the wheat market, and then the population, of the mid-Hudson Valley, as wheat and other produce from the west could now be shipped east.

The Hudson River sloops, once a common means of river transportation, were later replaced by steam boats. The sloops pictured here are in a harbor at Troy New York. New York State Council on the Arts portfolio for the Hudson River Sloop Restoration, Inc.

Chapter 10
DEVELOPMENT OF THE RAILROADS

In 1812, five years before the Erie Canal was begun and two years before the first locomotive was even built, Colonel John Stevens III, of Hoboken and Annadale, published a pamphlet promoting "The Superior Advantages of Railways and Steam Carriages Over Canal Navigation." In 1820, Stevens and his sons built a prototype steam locomotive that ran on a circular track—five years before George Stephenson, in England, put the first steam-powered railway train into business.[36] As Emerson wrote, "the Americans [took] to this little contrivance, the railroad, as if it were the cradle in which they were born." In 1840, there were fewer than 3,000 miles of railroad track in the country; by 1860, there were more than 30,000.

Hudson River Railroad

Inaugurated in 1846 and completed in 1851, the Hudson River Railroad (HRRR) ran between New York City and Albany, making stops at Rhinecliff. One of the first railroads in New York State, it brought radical changes to Rhinebeck and the Hudson Valley, ending the 50 years' service of the New York-Albany stagecoach and causing a drastic reduction in riverborne shipping. In 1869, the HRRR was consolidated within the New York Central Railroad, and more tracks were laid.

The original tunnel dug through the Astor property, north of Rhinecliff, is pictured in an early photograph. Rokeby Collection.

Train derailment south of Rhinecliff station, on the New York Central Line. March 13, 1912. Museum of Rhinebeck History.

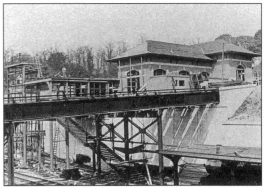

A railroad station was located at the foot of Shatzel Avenue until 1912. Museum of Rhinebeck History.

A new railroad station was built with the aid of John Jacob Astor and Levi P. Morton, whose private railroad cars were often left near the station. Museum of Rhinebeck History.

Local Newspapers

Life grew quicker, more mobile. People and goods traveled farther, faster and more easily, and so did mail and news. Rhinebeck's first newspaper, *The Rhinebeck Advocate,* was published in 1841; *The Rhinebeck Gazette* followed in 1846. Townspeople boasted they read the news at least one day before the people of Albany, since mail traveling up from the City was delivered to Rhinebeck first.

This masthead for The Rhinebeck Gazette was used during the last part of the nineteenth century. The paper was in operation from 1846 to 1969, when it was combined with the Red Hook Advertiser and became the Gazette Advertiser. Anniversary booklet, "The Rhinebeck Gazette" Rhinebeck Town Historian.

Delaware and Hudson Canal

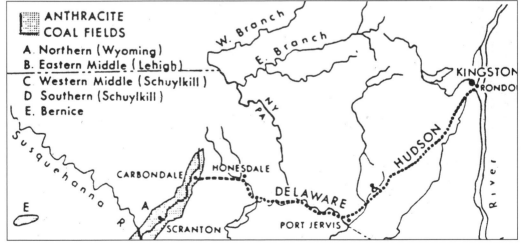

The Canal from Honesdale, Pennsylvania, brought coal to Rondout, a port with access to the Hudson. Map by the Army Corps of Engineers.

While the region's declining wheat market resulted in a drop in population, the drop was temporary, relieved in the latter half of the century in part by opportunities provided by the Delaware and Hudson Canal. Opened west of the Hudson in 1828, and enlarged in 1842 and 1851, the canal was originally intended to transport coal. (By the latter part of the century, however, it supported the growing cement industry as well.) The coal was loaded on barges and carried from Pennsylvania to Kingston, and then down river to New York City or across to Rhinecliff (the former Kipsbergen). There, it was transferred to cars on the Rhinebeck and Connecticut Railroad for the trip east into New England.

The Hucklebush Railroad

The Rhinebeck and Connecticut Railroad, completed in 1873, was known locally as the Hucklebush,[37] nicknamed for the berry bushes growing along its tracks. It carried produce and passengers, as well as coal, until it ceased operations July 1938. Although never itself a great financial success, the Hucklebush was the object of much local pride and affection. Stopping in the village of Rhinebeck at Hog Bridge (Montgomery Street and Mt. Rutsen Road), it supplied a vehicle for boyhood adventures and boosted commerce in the mid-Hudson Valley.

Crew at Rhinecliff pictured by the CNE engine #19. The train is facing east Rail service on the Rhinebeck & Connecticut Rail Raod began in 1873. Courtesy of R. W. Nimke.

Stationmaster John J. Creed is pictured at the Rhinebeck station, which was located at Hog Bridge at the north end of Montgomery Street. Courtesy of A. Coon.

A crew removes tracks of the "Hucklebush" railroad about 1939. The railroad ceased operation July 1938. Photo courtesy of Jack Swanberg.

After the railroad ceased operation, the Rhinebeck Station was moved several times. This photo, taken January 26, 1946, shows the station on Montgomery Street moving past the first Baptist church and Sinclair station. Asher Collection.

Irish Immigrants

Between 1830 and 1860, the nation's population more than doubled to more than 31 million. Approximately 1.5 million of those crossing the ocean to America were Irish, driven out from Ireland by impoverishment after the potato crop failed in 1845. A good number of Irish Catholics came to the Rhinebeck area settling south of Kipsbergen in Rhinecliff. This was near the railroad, where they found employment laying railway tracks, putting up buildings, and maintaining the trains. A hard-working and spirited people, they rioted more than once over disputes with the railroad management about pay. They also helped man the growing number of factories and served the families of the great houses.

Tin plate photographs shows unidentified laborers in Rhinecliff. Museum of Rhinebeck History.

Gradually they improved their lot, and bought their own homes and plots of land. They also established Rhinebeck's first Catholic church (in Rhinecliff, in 1864), and contributed yet another rich flavor to the local cultural stew.

Ice Industry

If steamboats were fast, trains were many times faster. While a steamboat could make the Rhinecliff-New York City round trip in 28 hours, it took the train only four hours one way. Commercial ventures not dreamed of before the invention of steamboat and rail suddenly sprang up and thrived. For example, farmers and other laborers found off-season jobs harvesting ice from the Hudson to provide refrigeration for buildings in New York City and, more importantly, for fresh foods as they were transported to other locations as far away as Asia and South America.[38] For interim storage there was a large ice house near Long Dock in Rhinecliff and another ice house on the banks of Crystal Lake, then known as Asher Pond.

Crew cutting Ice on Asher's Pond. Harvesting ice was big business for many years. Museum of Rhinebeck History.

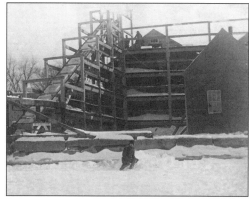

Ice houses were used to store the ice that was cut from the Hudson. In this picture, ice is placed on the conveyer (left) and place in the ice house, visible in the rear of the photo. Navins Collections.

Cutters would move snow away with teams of horses and wooden plows. Cutters then used hand saws, horse drawn devices or gasoline driven circular saws. Loaders moved ice from where it was cut to the endless chain elevator that lifted the ice blocks into storage houses. Probably the most undistinguished job during the ice harvest was cleaning up horse droppings from the ice field.[39]

The simple act of icing produce to keep it from spoilage meant that food no longer had to be grown close to those who consumed it. This fostered the change from an agrarian to a market-based economy and accelerated the process of centralization.

Frank Morgan, John Kimbark and Glen Manning display prize Guernsey cattle at Margaret Weaver's farm, east of Rhinebeck. This barn burned in September 1941 and was later rebuilt. Nancy Kelly Collection.

Rhinebeck Produce

As less wheat was harvested in the region, the Rhinebeck farmers took to fruit and dairy farming, sending their produce, milk, cream, and butter off on the early morning Hucklebush run. In this way, too, the trains encouraged new life in the town and region, forging the way to New York's dominance in finance and industry and eventually to its major role as manufacturer following the Industrial Revolution.

Rhinebeck Manufacturing

In 1861, Cyrus Morse founded the Union Iron Works in a building at the corner of Center and East Market streets. The company employed more than 150 men to work its steel and brass foundries. It produced such items as spinning machinery for the Harmony Mills at Cohoes and fixtures for the Episcopal church. The factory building later housed a sequence of other ventures, including the Little Monitor Sewing Machine Company (*c.* 1872), and a lumber business.

The Mill wheel near Route 9, Rhinebeck village. The upper mill, north of the bridge crossing the Landmans Kill was in operation for a century and a half. The abandoned mill wheel has long served as a symbol of industry in early Rhinebeck. Asher Collection.

Mill on the north of Asher's Pond (Crystal Lake) is shown before it burned. Dredging equipment is in the foreground. Asher Collection.

Early Enviromentalists

Not everyone was happy with the new life. Some saw the trains and other feats of engineering and manufacture as threatening to the Hudson Valley. The quarrying of slate for roofs, tiles, and billiard table tops exhausted the local quality supply by 1874. (The slate was borne by dray from the vicinity of Slate Quarry Road to the shipping point at Slate Dock in Rhinecliff. Slate Dock remained a major port for other shipments to and from New York City even after the failure of the slate business.) Saw mills and thick black smoke from locomotives also had their impact on the surroundings. The Romantics—the environmentalists of the mid-19th century—deplored what they saw as rampant materialism and the destruction of their wooded landscapes.

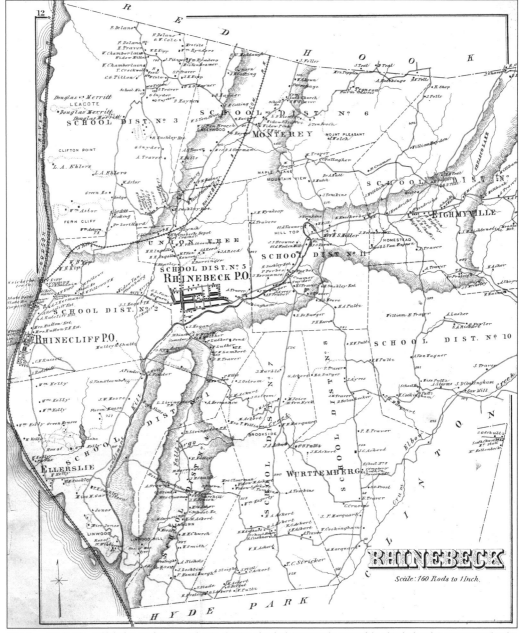

Map from Gray's Atlas, published at Reading, Pennsylvania, showing Rhinebeck in 1876. The route of the Rhinebeck and Connecticut Railroad is visible leading east from Rhinecliff and north from Rhinebeck. Museum of Rhinebeck History.

Chapter 11
CIVIL WAR (1861–1865)

*t*he Civil War broke out in April 1861. Abraham Lincoln had just been elected president in a Republican sweep that contributed to the defeat of Rhinebeck resident William Kelly, Democratic nominee for New York governor that year. En route to his inauguration in Washington, Lincoln traveled by train from Illinois through Rhinebeck. As the major port and economic center of the North, New York had a singular role to play in the four-year struggle, although no military action took place in the state.

Calvin Rikert, 128th Regiment, Company C, is shown in his Civil War uniform. Museum of Rhinebeck History.

The Draft

Both armies had trouble raising men to fight. The Union was impelled to pass the Conscription Act of 1863, which resulted in four days of anti-draft riots in New York City. Nonetheless, Dutchess County supplied most of the men of the 150th New York Volunteer Infantry Regiment, popularly called the Dutchess County Regiment Companies F, G, K, and B; the 128th Company C; 44th (People's Ellsworth Regiment); and the 20th Regiment of the New York State Militia. The Rhinebeckers who set off to war with the 150th Regiment carried a flag sewn for them by the ladies of the Dorcas Guild of the Dutch Reformed Church and a each carried a copy of the New Testament, a gift from Mrs. Stephen Olin, a Livingston and Beekman descendant. The flag was carried into the Battle of Gettysburg, at Chattanooga, at the siege of Atlanta, on Sherman's March to the Sea, and in the final campaign up through the Carolinas that brought the war to a close in 1865. The flag is one of Rhinebeck's historic treasures.

Certificate exempting Jacob Tremper from service in the Civil War due to his age. Rhinebeck Town Records.

Prisoners of War

Of the 115 or so Rhinebeck men who fought in the war, about 13 percent died.[40] Many of the survivors were wounded or spent time in Southern prisons. There, the prisoners would pass the time crafting things from cigar boxes and carving peach pits, or the officers among them might read to their men.

Members of the Grand Army of the Republic (GAR) marching in the Memorial Day parade, c. 1898. Rhinebeck Historical Society.

The musket and saber of Calvin Rikert(left). Museum of Rhinebeck History.
Grand Army of the Republic Rhinebeck Veterans gather for 50th anniversary(above). Caption on reverse of the photograph probably contained names of those pictured but is too faded to read. Museum of Rhinebeck History.

Lee's Surrender

After four years of bloody battle in which 600,000 lives were lost, Lee surrendered his army to Grant. The Union was restored. On April 11, 1864, "The Rhinebeck Gazette" reported:

The news of Lee's defeat and the capture of Richmond was received in our village on Monday night of last week and made our whole population delirious with joy… The Rhinebeck band paraded our streets, the people kindled bonfires, rang bells, shouted, fired crackers, cannons and guns, and in many other ways testified their joy at the good news.

Reverand David Hanaburgh pictured with carved peach pit and ring made while imprisoned during the Civil War (left). Flag made by the Dorcas Guild of the Dutch Reformed Church and carried by the 150th Regiment. Conservation, funded in memory of Chester Haen, has been used to preserve this important relic (right). Photo by Douglas Baz.

Pocahontas, 1859 hand pumper is still in working condition and has won many awards at competitions. It is pictured here about 1918 in front of the old fire house on West Market Street. DAR

The firehouse built on West Market Street in 1869 had a stately tower and bell that have been removed. Museum of Rhinebeck History.

A Disastrous Fire

Rhinebeck residents mistook the bell that rang on the morning of May 8, 1864, as a continuation of the end-of-war celebrations. It was intended, however, as a fire alarm. Some oil rags in a barrel had combusted, igniting a blaze that raged for a full two days and destroyed almost half the town's business district. A bucket brigade of men, women, and children formed a line from Landsmans Kill to East Market Street, joining those manning the hand pumper, known as "Old Pokie," to douse the flames.

Lincoln's Funeral Train

William Carroll, a furniture maker whose business also provided coffins and undertaker services advertized in The Rhinebeck Gazette. He is probably the mortician who repaired Lincoln's corpse at Rhinecliff. Museum of Rhinebeck History.

After the surrender, but before peace could be properly made, Lincoln was shot at Ford's Theater. His funeral train followed the same route home to Illinois by which he had first come to Washington four years before. The track at Rhinecliff was lined with mourners. Historian Dr. Henry Noble MacCracken believed that a stop was made at Rhinebeck to allow a local mortician to prepare the corpse for viewing in Albany.

Reconstruction

The first years of recovery after the Civil War were rocky in Rhinebeck and throughout the country; it was a time of manic highs and depressions. The first decade brought two brief but serious economic slumps, one a year after the end of the war and another in 1873. In between and after, a giddy ambition for wealth and personal power took over the town and the nation.

The town pump was a prominent sight in the center of the village. It was located on the corner near the Beekman Arms and replaced an earlier spring and watering trough, which probably had served since Indian times c.1897. Museum of Rhinebeck History.

Herrick Lumber Company occupied a building constructed in 1861 by Cyrus B. Morse to house the Union Iron Works. The village hall and firehouse now occupy the site. Asher Collection.

Gold Fever

Further fueling the feverish mood, in 1867, word got out that gold had been found near Welch's Cave, close to Lake Sepasco and the Sepascot tribe's original village. A burst of land sales followed. Gold mining companies were formed and a mine shaft was dug, but gold was not found in sufficient quantity to warrant the activity. A second "gold rush" occurred in 1884.[41]

The Civil War had helped usher in mass markets and mass production and unleashed on the country a new ethic in business. Contractors were overcharging the government for shoddy goods, carpetbaggers from the North were cleaning up in the South, and the great robber barons were growing fat building our railroads. Our young government had no provisions in its laws for the new kinds of business practices that were evolving with the new forms of business.

This shaft on Enterprise Road is the site of a gold mine that was operated from 1867 to 1868 by Dr. Martin Fraleigh and his son Edwin, and financed through stockholders. Photo by Douglas Baz.

Chapter 12
THE GILDED AGE

*t*he last two decades of the 19th century were golden ones for Rhinebeck. The town became known as the "Parlor of Dutchess."

Bank of Rhinebeck, incorporated 1853 was originally located at the "White Corner." It became the First National Bank in 1865. The building (1879) originally had a tower which has since been removed.

Rhinebeck Savings Bank, organized 1860. The first president was Joshua C. Bowne. The Savings Bank was built in 1884 with a tower which has been removed. Museum of Rhinebeck History.

Sleigh ride pictures Roger O'Dell with a turn of the century sleigh on Chestnut Street. Asher Collection.

Nineteen-hundred view of Mill Street looking south from the four corners of Rhinebeck. Museum of Rhinebeck History.

Grand Village Houses

The new prosperity was visible in Rhinebeck Village, where grand Victorian mansions were built by many of the newly rich. Each morning the streets were watered down to keep the dust settled as the horses and buggies went by.

Suddenly there were opportunities for making money that had not existed before. A new generation of prosperous and prominent men, having made quick fortunes in New York City, came upstate to build their own country estates along the bank of the Hudson, in or near Rhinebeck. As many as 12 trains a day carried these commuters up from the city, making scheduled stops at Rhinecliff Station. There, lined up on the side rails and fitted out with every latest luxury, private railroad cars awaited the use of their wealthy owners.

Home of John O'Brien, a successful Irishman, who was a contractor for the Rhinebeck and Connecticut Railroad and member of the New York State Assembly. The house, located on the corner of Livingston and Mulberry streets, was designed by Gilbert B. Croft and built in 1876. It was the first in the village to be illuminated by gas. Quitman Resource Center National Register Survey.

This house at 43 Livingston Street was originally constructed by Henry Latson, circa 1870. It featured a tower that has since been removed. He lived in the house until his death in 1885. Quitman Resource Center National Register Survey

Ambrose Wager was a prominent attorney, town supervisor, and member of the New York State Assembly. His house, designed by Gilbert B. Croft, was built in 1873 on West Market Street. Quitman Resource Center National Register Survey.

House on West Market Street owned by members of the Kiersted, Heermance, Teller and Wells families. The earliest section was built in 1793; the impressive tower and additions were built later. Museum of Rhinebeck History.

Lost Victorians

Victorian and Gilded Age embellishments such as towers, cupolas and gingerbread, greeted the eye in Rhinebeck before World War I. They were eagerly torn away to "modernize" buildings or the buildings were removed to make way for progress. The result was a major loss. Rhinebeck must have looked very grand when its many important houses lined the main streets.

The George Tremper house occupied the lot that later became the Rhinebeck Chevy Garage property. This large Victorian was the Rhinebeck Post Office before 1939. Museum of Rhinebeck History.

Dr. Platt's house was located between the Episcopal church and the original Baptish church. It was demolished to build the gas station which now occupies the site.

House on the site of Ruge's Oldsmobile. The automobile dealership was built in front of the house and the house used for temporary schoolrooms from 1939 to 1952. Rhinebeck Historical Society.

Mrs. Freeborn Garrettson, widow of the nephew of the Reverend Garrettson, owned this house on the site of the present Rhinebeck Animal Hospital. Courtesy of Don Kallop.

Corner of East Market and Montgomery streets shows the Shaffer Store, a grocery that burned and was replaced with Al Stickle's Five & Dime (top left). VonderLinden building was built in 1868 after the town fire; brick has stood the test of time (top right).

White Corner was torn down in September 1940 to make way for a gas station. View shows the building fronting on West Market with Montgomery and the present Foster's Coach House to the right (bottom left).

View shows the Beekman Arms, then the Rhinebeck Hotel, with Victorian porches. Town pump is in the foreground (bottom right). Museum of Rhinebeck History.

Buildings on the northeast corner in Rhinebeck remain much the same, except for the A. L. Stickle building (top left).

View looking up East Market Street shows the fine row of brick buildings built after the Civil War, which replaced those lost in the fire (top right).

The gas station that stood on the northwest corner for fifty years is gone now, replaced with a well-landscaped parking lot (bottom left).

Tracy Dows bought the Beekman Arms and renovated it in 1917, removing the Victorian porches and applying a Mt. Vernon treatment to its facade. Architect Harrie T. Lindeberg's design is similar to his Fox Hollow Mansion plan (bottom right). Photos by Douglas Baz.

Chapter 13
THE ESTATES

O n June 28, 1890, *The Rhinebeck Gazette* noted, "Rhinebeck has more millionaires for a little county town than any other place of its size in the country," and then proceeded to name them—Astor, Delano, Merritt, Cruger, Morton, Suckley, Dinsmore, Huntington, Livingston, Wager, Wells, Miller, O'Brien, among others. Many of these left an enduring stamp on Rhinebeck's landscape, history and community.

Ferncliff—The Astors

Ferncliff *mansion on river Road, was built by William Backhouse Astor and occupied by his son, John Jacob Astor and grandson Vincent Astor before being demolished after World War II c. 1915.* Museum of Rhinebeck History.

Gatehouse at Ferncliff *was designed by E. H. Ehlers. Large Astor greenhouses were located nearby. Photo, S. Lichens c. 1989.* Quitman Resource Center, National Register Survey

The Astor family has exerted an influence on Rhinebeck life from the early 19th century to the present day. The family's founder was John Jacob Astor, who made his fortune in fur trade and from New York City real estate. His son, William Backhouse Astor, married the daughter of Alida Livingston Armstrong and inherited Rokeby. John Jacob's grandson, William Backhouse Astor Jr. (1830-1892), established the family seat at Ferncliff, one of the largest Rhinebeck riverfront properties. There William's son, John Jacob Astor IV (1864-1912), was born. Before his untimely death, John Jacob ("Jack") invented a number of useful devices and gathered up 2,800 acres of real estate around Rhinebeck Village. His land purchasing activities provoked concern, however; local businessmen feared that the town was in danger of a takeover. Five prominent citizens, including Dr. George N. Miller, one of Rhinebeck's millionaires cited in the "Gazette" article on that subject, organized the Rhinebeck Realty Corporation to purchase land on the town's behalf.

One of the aims of Rhinebeck Realty was to purchase property to resell at a lower price to those otherwise unable to afford it. The company also lent money for repairs and building and, in 1930, donated land to the Northern Dutchess Health Service Center, founded by Dr. Miller, for building their new hospital.

William B. Astor Jr. (1830–1892) established the family seat at Ferncliff. Rokeby Collection.

John Jacob Astor IV (1846–1912) greatly expanded the Ferncliff *land holdings.* Rokeby Collection.

In addition to overseeing the family interests, the Astors invested considerable energy and resources in philanthropic pursuits on behalf of the Rhinebeck community, as well as New York City and State. William Backhouse Astor Sr. who established the Astor Library (now New York Public Library), also built an orphanage and church in Red Hook. Generations of Astors hosted the Rhinebeck townsfolk each year for a Fourth of July fireworks display at *Ferncliff.* Jack financed a light artillery company that saw action in the Spanish-American War and offered his yacht, *The Nourmahal,* for the war effort. Through the efforts of Jack and former Governor Levi P. Morton, a most elegant railroad station house was completed at Rhinecliff in 1913. When Jack went down with the *Titanic,* his funeral was held at the Church of the Messiah in Rhinebeck and received national attention. His son, Vincent, then took over *Ferncliff* and kept it up until his death in 1959.

In honor of his father, Vincent founded Holiday Farm for children from city slums in 1915; the facility was turned into an orphanage, the Astor Home for Children, in 1953. Upon breaking up the *Ferncliff* estate in 1964, Vincent's widow Brooke donated to the town 196 acres of land, Ferncliff Forest, to be kept forever wild. Other lands were donated to The Archbishopric of New York as a site for the Ferncliff Nursing Home.

Astor Home for Children, interior view, from the Dows photograph collection. Begun by Mary Morton as Holiday Farm in 1909, the home was purchased by Vincent Astor in 1914 and moved to Rhinebeck where a Tudor-style building was designed by Harrie T. Lindeberg. Asher Collection.

Indoor pool at Ferncliff *was part of a building design by Stanford White.* Dows Collection.

Ellerslie—Levi P. Morton

This Tudor-style mansion, circa 1889, replaced the earlier William Kelly mansion on this estate south of Rhinecliff. It burned in 1950 while occupied by the Cardinal Farley Military Academy. Museum of Rhinebeck History.

Levi Parsons Morton was another of Rhinebeck's millionaires. He was a former congressman and minister to France, and in that role, accepted the Statue of Liberty given by France to the United States, July 4, 1884. He moved to *Bois Dore*—today the site of the Astor Home—in 1888, the same year he was elected vice-president under Benjamin Harrison. Later he moved his family to a newly built mansion, *Ellerslie,* on the site of William Kelly's former home known by the same name. Elected governor of New York in 1894, Morton took an active part in Rhinebeck life, donating the Morton Memorial Library to the town. His daughter donated a pipe organ and a stained glass window to the Church of the Messiah in Rhinebeck. On his birthday each year he gave a party at his home for the children of Rhinecliff. He turned *Ellerslie* into a model farm, which his daughter and heir eventually donated to the Catholic Archdiocese of New York in 1946. Between 1942 and 1971, the property served as the campus for the well known Cardinal Farley Military Academy. Recently, it served as a home for troubled youths, called Holy Cross, and as the campus for the Rhinecliff Union Free School. Holy Cross has now been closed.

Wilderstein—The Suckleys

Thomas Suckley, a Beekman descendant who made his fortune in New Jersey real estate, built *Wilderstein,* an elaborate Victorian estate on part of Freeborn Garrettson's former property. His son Robert employed Arnout Cannon Jr. to rebuild the earlier house according to a design in the Queen Anne style. He then had it landscaped by Calvert Vaux, who created Central Park in New York City.

Original house built by Thomas Suckley, circa1853, at Wilderstein *was designed by John Warren Ritch in the Italianate villa style.* Museum of Rhinebeck History.

Margaret "Daisy" Suckley posing on the south lawn of Wildercliff. Photo by Eric Kreiger. Courtesy of Times Herald Record

In 1983, Robert's daughter Margaret ("Daisy"), cousin and confidante of Franklin Roosevelt, donated the property to the Wilderstein Preservation, a not-for-profit preservation group.

Wildercliff, *home of Catherine Livingston and the Reverand Freeborn Garrettson included property which was later deeded to the Suckely family for the* Wilderstein *estate.*

An interior shot of the Wildercliff *dining room.*

Foxhollow—The Dowses

Tracy Dows of *Foxhollow* served as a director of several Rhinebeck institutions, including the Dutchess Light, Heat and Power Company; the Rhinebeck Savings Bank; and the Red Hook Phone Company. He bought and renovated the Beekman Arms, and maintained it as a central focal point for the community. Thomas Wolfe visited the Dowses at their colonial revival home in 1925 and described the family in his novel, *Of Time and the River*. Today *Foxhollow* houses Daytop Village, an organization dedicated to rehabilitation from substance abuse.

Preparing for a foxhunt at Foxhollow. Harrie T. Lindeberg designed the house for Tracy Dows. Thomas Wolfe visited here when he and the Dowses' son, Olin, were students at Harvard. Museum of Rhinebeck History.

Chapter 14
PROGRESS

*b*y the beginning of the 20th century, social and economic inequities created by post-Civil War industrial expansion and laissez faire policy were glaring. A movement for reform, Progressivism, gathered momentum to protect the rights of workers and farmers and address the abuses of private power.

"Up in the Air about Rhinebeck," etching by Edwin Marquart in 1913, shows the outdoor theatre with a tall pine tree on West Market Street. Museum of Rhinebeck History.

O'Dell Market on East Market Street was probably a grocery store. Museum of Rhinebeck History.

Water wagon, shown near Center Street on East Market Street, sprinkled the village streets to keep down the summer dust. Rhinebeck Historical Society.

Social Change

The focus of New York's social scene shifted away from the Beekman-Livingston heirs and the Hudson Valley to the nouveaux rich and their places in Newport and on Long Island. Sports joined farming and horticulture as the leisure pursuits of choice. There began in the region a slow decline of the river places, fueled by the newly instituted income tax and the increasing cost of estate maintenance that persisted through the century.

Utilities

At the end of the 19th century, Rhinebeck homes were heated with coal and many were still lit with kerosene lamps. Others used gas until the Dutchess Light, Heat and Power Company opened for business on Montgomery Street in 1900. There was little indoor plumbing; many still took their baths in kitchen tubs with water warmed on the stove.

A new office was constructed for the Dutchess Light Heat and Power Company north of the Rhinebeck Savings Bank on Montgomery Street. It later became the Central Hudson Building.

Public Water Works

In 1899, Rhinebeck inaugurated a public water system, the Rhinebeck Public Water Works. It supplied water from a reservoir on Burger Hill fed by gravity to the village. This considerably improved sanitation in the village. However, the water supply depended on wells, and it often had to be rationed during dry spells. Only in 1968, when the municipal water system was linked to the Hudson River and a filtration and pumping plant was installed at Rhinecliff, was the village assured of all the fresh water it would need.

Rhinebeck Water Company building at Long Dock, today. Photo by Douglas Baz.

Telephone

The first telephones came to Rhinebeck some time in the last two decades of the 19th century, though exactly when is not known. The wiring system was unsightly and highly unstable in storms. In 1909, Peter Troy of Barrytown, originally a telegrapher who then founded the Red Hook Telephone Company, bought out the local Rhinebeck company. The Red Hook company continued to service Rhinebeck until 1971, when a national company took over.

The old telephone building on Mill Street was replaced by a large brick structure in 1977. It is now occupied by offices and shops. Asher collection.

Violet Industry

At the end of the century, Rhinebeck grew sweet violets. For 40 years, beginning in 1890, Rhinebeck grew so many violets it came to be known as "The Violet Capital of the World." The fashion of the day was such that "young women wore [violets] almost exclusively... A boy dare not ask the girl of his choice to a football game without going into debt for some pounds of violets."[42] The land off Rock City Road belonging to George Saltford, the man who first brought the violet to town from his brother's greenhouse in Poughkeepsie, became known as Violet Hill. By 1907, violets were the main source of revenue for Dutchess County, bringing in more than one million dollars per year. Almost half the homes in the village of Rhinebeck had a greenhouse or two growing violets. Julius Von der Linden had 64 violet houses; he was the first "Violet King." At one time there were so many glass greenhouses of violets that the reflection of the sun's rays upon them caused the town to be called "Crystal City."

Violet shipments began in the fall and culminated with the Easter season. At the height of the season, schools closed to allow students time to pick and bunch the flowers. Violet Hill, Violet Avenue and Violet Place recall the volume of flowers grown and shipped.

But as quickly as it had come, the violet craze faded. The flimsy clothing of the Flappers in the 1920s could not support heavy bunches of violets. Fashion turned to roses, camellias, gardenias, chrysanthemums, and then orchids. By 1918, the Rhinebeck violet industry was on the wane; by 1930 it was disappearing. A few growers continued until the fuel crisis of 1976. In 1979 the last violet house closed. Today the town grows anemones.

View east, down Chestnut Street from the steeple of the Episcopal Church, showed some of the many greenhouses located in Rhinebeck village. Tremper Collection.

Violet workers spent long hours stretched on narrow boards, planting and then picking the crop. A majority of the population found some employment in the violet industry. Museum of Rhinebeck History.

Chapter 15
THE GREAT WAR

When war broke out in Europe in 1914 it was not of immediate concern to most Americans. We were an ocean away from the action. But the Germans kept sinking our merchant ships and other unarmed ships on which Americans were sailing. In April 1917, we declared war on Germany, committed to fighting for international law and "to make the world safe for democracy." Then the war became of concern to everyone.

"Home Defense" gathered for training at the Dutchess County Fairgrounds. They were all local men, prepared to leave their jobs or businesses whenever needed. For a time, guns were scarce so the troops trained with brooms. Museum of Rhinebeck History.

First War Efforts

In Rhinebeck, barrels were set out on Main Street to collect walnut shells for the manufacture of ammunition. Rhinebeckers saved twine and tinfoil, knit washcloths and sweaters, rolled bandages, and sewed. They ran rallies at which war bonds, coffee and doughnuts were sold, all to support their country's fighting men. Again, an Astor yacht was sent to war.

As was the case in towns throughout the country, families of German origin, of which there were many in Rhinebeck, immediately came under suspicion, no matter their citizenship or politics. At the high school they stopped teaching German and offered French classes instead.

A World War I plane on the lawn of the Beekman Arms recalls the heroic pilots of the era. This photograph was staged to advertise an air show that took place at the Cozine Airport on the southeast side of the village. Museum of Rhinebeck History.

Rhinebeck's Fighting Forces

A force of 500,000 American men was deployed to Europe under General Pershing. They joined the Meuse-Argonne offensive of 1918 that led to the Germans' retreat and the end of hostilities. Rhinebeck sent 179 men to fight in the war; eight of those men died. Plaques are placed to their memory in Rhinebeck 's Town Hall and on a boulder in the Rhinecliff Memorial Park.

The World War I doughboy was purchased by Dewitt Gurnell, 1972, in honor of the Rhinebeck men who fought in the wars. (left) The statue was restored in 1999 and placed in front of the municipal parking lot. Museum of Rhinebeck History. *A bond fundraising parade was held April 1918. The Liberty Coach is shown with the White Corner in the background and Beekman Arms at the left. Photo by Alan Coon.*

Treaty of Versailles

After the war, in the Treaty of Versailles, our European allies imposed on the Germans terms of such harshness that ill-feelings festered. Meanwhile, the Americans retreated behind their isolationist policy to their pursuit of prosperity and to what President Harding called "normalcy." As Rhinebecker Fannie Sipperley wrote in her journal, "It was as if the war had never been."[43]

The Liberty Ball followed the Liberty Coach to Rhinebeck in April of 1918 for the Third Liberty Loan Drive. Dows Collection.

The Judson building, "Schemmy's," is shown decked out with bunting. The building was the home of the Odd Fellows Hall. Museum of Rhinebeck History.

Chapter 16
BETWEEN THE WARS

*t*he war revolutionized manufacturing and the economy in this country. While before the war automobiles were scarce, they were everywhere after war.

Influence of the Automobile

Automobiles necessitated the building of garages and the paving of roads. In Rhinebeck, garages replaced some Victorian houses. Automobiles accelerated what had been begun by the trains, changing Rhinebeck from a self-contained farming community into a rural retreat for those making their livelihoods elsewhere.

The White Corner was replaced with an Esso service station owned by George Bravinger. Asher Collection.

The gas station replaced Dr. Platt's house between the Episcopal Church and the original Baptist church on Montgomery Street. Asher Collection.

The Hub Garage on Mill Street, Rhinebeck c. 1922 showing left to right: John Donaldson, Mort Sullivan, Harry Rynders, Wilfield Bathrick, Dick Turton, Ralph Wheeler, Peter Snyder, Clarence Rynders, an unknown man, and Gus Ebers. Museum of Rhinebeck History.

The Djinis' Rhinebeck Diner, south of the bank on Mill Street was a classic, attracting travelers from New York to Albany. Asher Collection.

Our Agricultural Backbone

Throughout Rhinebeck's history, agriculture has played a large part in the town's economy. The farms evolved from self-subsistent units and became major wheat producers. Later farms produced dairy and other products which could supply the large population in New York City. In the early 1900s, apple orchards could be found on many farms and many barrels of apples were shipped to the city.

This 1861 view of the barn at Ellerslie is an example of the serious farming that took place on the estates. Rokeby Collection.

Silos and barns west of Rhinebeck Village, owned by the Astors, is now the site of The Gardens condominiums.

Patrons of Husbandry, Rhinebeck Grange No. 345, was organized in November 1900. The brick grange hall is pictured in May 1941. It is now an office building. Asher Collection.

Sickle bar mower with a team of horses was used from the time of the industrial revolution until the coming of the gas tractor. Walter Vogel is shown riding the mower and guiding the team. Museum of Rhinebeck History.

Summer Boarders

Farm wives augmented the family income by "taking in summer people." Train and automobile transportationn made it possible for city families to vacation in the country. Some came and spent the summer while the breadwinner commuted on weekends; others took a vacation week or two in the country air, enjoying the bountiful food provided by the farm wife and the pleasant scenery and peaceful atmosphere. Many area houses were crowded with temporary residents during the summer season.

(from left to right) Rhinebeck postcard seems to encourage visitors. Fred Briggs Collection. *The Mohrman farm on Route 9G was typical of the many farms which accommodated boarders for the summer. It was redesigned after a fire destroyed the second floor.* Museum of Rhinebeck History. *It is now the Buttonwood Farm. Staley Cottage, located on Mt. Rutsen Road, within easy walking distance of the village and the Hog Bridge Station, was a popular tourist location.* Museum of Rhinebeck History.

Prohibition

Resentment of German brewers, among other factors, contributed to the passing of Prohibition in 1919. Rhinebeck had its share of strict observers of Prohibition law, as well as its share of rum runners. Some local residents did a fair business in homemade applejack. A ditty popular at the time declared:

> Oh, we're from Dutchess County
> and we would like to have you know
> that we're from Dutchess County
> where the luscious apples grow.
> They call us apple knockers, but
> really we're not that,
> because we're from Dutchess County
> Where they make the applejack.

The law stayed on the books, although perhaps not always enforced, until 1933.

Improved Communications

Telephones and radios did for communication what the railroads and automobiles had done for transportation. The world was becoming much bigger and smaller at the same time.

Operator Minerva Bravinger and her sister Marie shown at the telephone switchboard in Rhinebeck c. 1939. Museum of Rhinebeck History.

Klan Activity

In reaction to the strength of the pre-war reform movement, the first years after the war returned people's focus to the pursuit of affluence and away from the moral concerns of the Progressives. In Dutchess County, the Ku Klux Klan gathered strength. A cross was burned in Rhinecliff protesting the presidential candidacy of Catholic Al Smith.

The Depression

The 1920s were called "The Decade of Prosperity," or the wild and reckless "Jazz Age," although not everyone was able to be wild and reckless. While industry flourished, the farms suffered. Unemployment was high; wealth was shared only among a privileged few. The economy expanded, but too quickly. In the last years of the 1920s, the stock market showed signs of instability. In October 1929, it crashed.

The Depression hit hard in the mid-Hudson Valley, as in most small-town and rural areas. Rhinebeck's population decreased by more than 15 percent between 1910 and 1930.[44] The Depression also hit hard in Europe, as the economies of Europe and the United States were more closely linked than people had understood or wanted to recognize.

Dedication ceremony for the Rhinebeck Post Office took place on the front porch in 1939. Mrs. Roosevelt and FDR's mother both have large violet nosegays on their laps. Asher Collection.

Marching band in the 1940 Memorial Day parade. Asher Collection.

FDR's New Deal

In 1932, the country elected Franklin Roosevelt, a scion of Dutchess County, as its president. Roosevelt initiated the Works Progress Administration (WPA) to get people back to work and taking home paychecks. WPA projects in Rhinebeck included the building of Routes 9G and 308. Route 9G replaced the Wurtemburg

Road as the north-south route in the eastern part of town, and Route 308 was an improved road to Rock City. The WPA also built a new post office, a replica of the earliest portion of the Hendrick Kip house, using stone from the Kip-Beekman Herrmance house ruins and complete with murals depicting scenes from Rhinebeck history, painted by local artist Olin Dows. The post office's dedication in 1939 was a gala event attended by the president, the postmaster general, the secretary of the Treasury, and Crown Prince Frederik of Denmark.

President Roosevelt wanted the post office to be located near the historic Beekman Arms, and as a result, the town was convinced to allow the town hall on Mill Street to be torn down to make way for the post office. A new town hall was built through the WPA on East Market Street.

Ben Franklin Store on East Market Street c. 1943. Alfred and Jan Stickle purchased the business after World War II. The buildings were demolished to build the Savings Bank Shopping Plaza. Asher Collection.

Chapter 17
WORLD WAR II

Severe war reparations and the Great Depression combined to make Germany ripe for despotism; before Europe had fully recovered from World War I, it was fighting again. America tried to keep her distance, but again, our sunken ships—this time at Pearl Harbor—impelled us to take action. President Roosevelt, in 1941, stated "We must begin the great task that is before us, by abandoning once and for all the illusion that we can ever again isolate ourselves from the rest of humanity."[45]

Rhinebeck's Armed Forces

Jeeps parked near the Beekman Arms were part of a bond drive fund-raising effort. Asher Collection.

Rhinebeck sent 412 men and women to join the American Forces and help win an Allied victory. Seventeen were killed: Arthur C. Briggs, Henry C. Challis, Frederick T. Corey, Austin S. Frost Jr., Neil Gardner, John Gemmel, Carl E. Hoffman, Edwin V. Kerr, Louis Gordon Lown, David S. Lattin, Edson McCord, William J. McCue, Jr., Robert F. Miller, Raymond M. Pink, Roland Q. Traudt, Barrett L. Tyler, and Donald C. Whelpley.[46]

Home Defense

Reverend Fred Fatum of the Baptist Church broadcast religious services on the radio. A service flag, prominently displayed behind the group, notes church members in the service. Asher Collection.

Individuals participated in black-out drills, monitored by Air Raid Wardens, as part of home defense activities. "Airplane spotters" used a building set up three miles east of the village on Sharpe's farm and later a tower at Ferncliff Forest. Rationing of commodities such as sugar, tires and gasoline required registration and the use of rationing books. Scrap recycling efforts included a community scrap pile and Boy Scout newspaper collections. In addition families grew victory gardens and a special community garden project was set up at the future school grounds for 100 gardens. War bond and war stamp sale drives were held. The Flat Rock School on Rhinecliff Road received an award for participation of 90 percent of the school children who bought war stamps regularly.

No More Isolation

When the war ended, the shattering of the illusion of isolation became evident in small towns throughout the country, including Rhinebeck. No longer was the town with its shops, small businesses, and farms, an independent, more or less self-sufficent unit. No longer was its land used primarily for farming, but once again the town adjusted to major change and found a way to prosper.

The American Legion was given land by Robert and Ford Huntington to provide a park in memory of those who served in the war. It is now owned and maintained by the village. Members of the Legion are shown on the steps of the Church of the Messiah, Memorial Day 1947. Asher Collection.

Rhinebeck students pose in front of town scrap pile that they helped collect as a part of the war effort. Asher Collection.

A boulder placed in the Memorial Park in Rhinecliff honors the servicemen from that locality. Museum of Rhinebeck History.

Chapter 18
TODAY'S RHINEBECK

Since the 1940s, Rhinebeck's population has continued to grow. Its economy, now primarily commercial, has come to depend IBM for more than 50 years. The opening of the Kingston-Rhinecliff bridge in 1957 made the town even more accessible to commuters, for whom it serves as a bedroom community.

Bob Milroy participated in the 1952 Rhinebeck Community Day. Museum of Rhinebeck History.
Leonard Tremper is shown with a three wheeled chaise which may been the vehicle made in France for Janet Montgomery and ordered for her by Chancellor Livingston. It later became the property of her sister Catherine, wife of Reverand Freeborn Garrettson. Museum of Rhinebeck History.

The Starr Institute, founded in 1862 by Mrs. Mary R. Miller, granddaughter of General Philip Schuyler. The building served Rhinebeck's literary, community and recreational needs until 1975. Today it houses shops and the Upstate Film Theater, often combining lectures with films—continuing to provide an educational aspect to Rhinebeck life.

The Judson (Schemmy's) building 's ironwork trim, was obscured by an art deco facade in the 40's. It now has the original facade restored. Quitman Resource Center National Register Survey.

The new Rhinebeck firehouse is located on East Market Street and also houses the village hall. Photo by Douglas Baz.

The old firehouse on East Market Street has been converted into shops. Museum of Rhinebeck History.

The Rhinebeck Town Hall, built in 1869 on Mill Street, was demolished to make way for the post office building which now occupies the site. Asher Collection.

The Rhinebeck Savings Bank Plaza on East Market Street offers convenient parking and shops. Photo by Douglas Baz.

The new town hall was built on East Market Street in 1939. Asher Collection.

Dutchess County Fair

The Dutchess County Fair is located at Springbrook, once the farm of Thomas Reed, a Rhinebeck businessman. Photo by Douglas Baz.

The Dutchess County Fair, begun in 1845 and today one of the most important fairs in New York State, is held yearly by the County Agricultural Society during the third week of August. It has taken place at Rhinebeck's Springbrook Park since 1919. The fair made national headlines when Dutchess county residents Franklin Roosevelt and Thomas Dewey visisted annually during their terms as governor. Today, the fairgrounds also serve as the location for other popular events throughout the year.

Old Rhinebeck Aerodrome

The Old Rhinebeck Aerodrome, a museum of early airplanes, just across the town line in Red Hook, founded by Cole Palen, offers flying shows of vintage planes three seasons a year and attracts visitors from all over the world. It is reminiscent of Cozine Field, the airport located near Rhinebeck's Chancellor Livingston Elementary School in the first half of the 20th century. It was a fueling stop for mail planes. Many local pilots received training there.

Museum of Rhinebeck History

The Rhinebeck Museum, founded in 1992, offers revolving exhibits chronicling the history of the town. Its permanent exhibits include Indian arrow heads and items depicting the various periods of Rhinebeck history.

The Adams Memorial Chapel at the Rhinebeck Cemetery Association was the site of the first Rhinebeck museum, founded by town historian, Dewitt Gurnell. Exhibits were dismantled when the cemetery needed the building for caretaker's quarters. Quitman Resource Center National Register Survey.

Dewitt Gurnell (1909-1988), shown here in his familiar role as druggist, was the first official Rhinebeck town historian. He organized many community events, founded the Rhinebeck Historical Society and began a Rhinebeck Museum. The successor to this museum is now located at the Quitman House, north of the village on Route 9. Town Historian's Collection.

Governor Thomas Dewey and his wife visiting the Dutchess County Fair in 1945. Asher Collection.

The Kingston-Rhinecliff bridge, as seen from the Kingston side, was opened to traffic on February 2, 1957. Photo by Len Vogler.

The Rhinebeck Town Landing on the Hudson, formerly the Rhinecliff-Kingston ferry slip, is now used for a variety of pleasure boats and water sports. The Kingston-Rhincliff bridge, that put the ferry out of business, can be seen in the distance. Photo by Robert Kalman.

Preparing to take off for a World War I flying exhibition at the Old Rhinebeck Aerodrome.

Ice boating can still be seen on the Hudson. The Vixen, left, once owned by President Franklin Delano Roosevelt's family, now belongs to Reid Bielenberg of Germantown. The Rip Van Winkle is owned by the J. W. Aldrich family of Barrytown. Thomas Brener, Museum of Rhinebeck History, 1981.

Chapter 19
EDUCATION THROUGH THE YEARS

rhinebeck's first school shared a roof with its first church, the one the Palatines built in 1715 at Wey's Crossing Road. Even in 1814, when Rhinebeck's district school system was formally organized, the Wurtemburg and Stone Church schools were located on church property, evidence of the Lutheran Church's interest in education for children of its members. In the intervening years, neighborhood schools served the community. These were one-room structures, often with only one teacher each and only the simplest furnishings. By 1844, the town had 12 such schoolhouses, situated so that no Rhinebeck child would have to walk more than two miles each way for schooling. Many of those structures were still in service at the beginning of the 20th century. The Stone Church Schoolhouse is the only one remaining today that has not been converted into a dwelling

Rhinebeck Academy/DeGarmo Institute

The Rhinebeck Academy, offering a private classical education, was established in 1840 by a Methodist clergyman. The academy became the De Garmo Institute in 1860 when Professor James M. DeGarmo acquired the school. It became a highly reputed institution for local and boarding students.

Professor James M. DeGarmo bought the Rhinebeck Academy on Livingston Street in 1860 to provide quality education at the boarding school. From "Biographical History of Dutchess County" by Beers.

Revered Robert Scott, founder of the Baptist Church in Rhinebeck, built this lovely Greek Revival house on East Market Street. From about 1800, he conducted a classical boarding school at this site. Robert Colgate and James Stokes were among his students. He was offered the presidency of Colgate University by his former student but declined the honor. Photo by Douglas Baz.

District Schools

Rhinebeck children were educated in district schools, built within walking distance of their homes. Each district's board of trustees hired the teacher and provided a building with facilities and supplies. Families of the district often supplied firewood for use at the schoolhouse, boarded the teacher, and helped with the building of a new schoolhouse when necessary. Taxes were assessed for the teacher's pay but the budget was small.

Morton School, District 1, was located at the corner of Morton and Mill roads. The building was financed by the Garrettson family and probably designed by A. J. Davis. Asher Collection.

Brick School, District 2, was built in 1878 to serve the Rhinecliff community. It had many more rooms than other districts in the town. Asher Collection.

Hook School, District 3, was located on River Road and served students on River Road and Hook Road. Asher Collection.

The Hillside School, District 4, was located on the east side of Route 9, south of Rhinebeck Village. Asher Collection.

The Village School, District 5, combined school districts within the village. The first section was built in 1870 after much controversy. Museum of Rhinebeck History.

Stone Church School, District 6, is the only schoolhouse in the district that has not been converted to a residence. It was built on church land, south of St. Peter's Lutheran Church on Route 9. Asher Collection.

The Acker Hook School, District 7, was near the intersection of Ackert Hook and Primrose Hill Roads. Asher Collection.

Wurtemburg School, District 8, was built to the north of St Paul's Lutheran Church, on church land. Asher Collection.

Eighmeyville School, District 9, is located on Turnpike Road. Greek Revival influence can be noted in the architecture. School trustees' minutes from 1814 to 1940 are in the Daughters of the American Revolution collection of historical documents. Asher Collection.

District 10 school located at the corner of White Schoolhouse and Slate Quarry Roads. Asher Collection.

Miller School, District 11, shows the same architectural influence as the Morton School. It is located on the north side of Route 308. Asher Collection.

Flat Rock School, District 12, with a hipped roof, displays a different architectural style from the other schools in town. It was located on Rhinecliff Road between Rhinecliff and Rhinebeck. Asher Collection.

Village Union School

In 1870, Rhinebeck Union Free School for the elementary grades was built at Mulberry and East Market Street, consolidating several of the district schools. A high school was opened at the same location in 1900 to serve the whole village. The building was destroyed by fire in 1939.

Centralization

The Rhinebeck school building burned April 1939. Various factors prevented the community from building a new school for 11 years during which time the children were taught in temporary facilities. Dows Collection.

Taxpayers' disagreements about costs delayed centralization of the Rhinebeck schools until 1950. In 1951, the Rhinebeck Central School was built—with stones from the Astor estate—and thereafter students from all parts of town were picked up by bus to attend.

The Rhinebeck Central School was built in 1951, finally freeing students from one room schools and cramped temporary quarters which had existed since the school fire of 1939.

Schools Come and Go

The Chancellor Robert R. Livingston Elementary School was opened in 1967, and Rhinebeck High School was expanded in 1997 with its Bulkeley wing, housing the middle school.

In 1998, the old Bulkeley Middle School in the center of the village was sold to the Catholic Diocese to be used as the Father Brogan Spiritual Center.

The First Baptist Church sponsored the building of the Northern Dutchess Christian School for pre-kindergarten through eighth grade in 1980. It is now located in Red Hook.

The old Bulkeley School has taken on new life as the Father Brogen Spiritual Center of the Catholic church. Photo by Douglas Baz.

The Starr Institute

The Starr Institute was founded in 1866 by Mrs. Mary R. Miller (a granddaughter of General Schuyler) as a memorial to her late husband, Congressman William Starr Miller. Although not a school, it offered educational facilities to Rhinebeck residents at its building on Montgomery Street. These included a lecture room, reading room, circulating and reference libraries, and a room for ladies' circles. In 1907, the facility was expanded to house a branch of the YMCA; later a movie theater and indoor swimming pool were added. In 1975, a new library and recreation center was built on West Market Street, and the original Starr Institute building was sold. Today it is home to shops and the Upstate Films theater.

The Starr Library built on W. Market street. Starr Library, on West Market Street was built in 1975 after an extensive fund raising effort chaired by Mrs. Silas Frazer and Mrs. Clarence Howe. The Thompson Trust matched funds to enable the new recreation center and expanded library to become a reality. It is the successor to the Starr Institute. Museum of Rhinebeck History.

Upstate Films

Upstate Films, begun in 1972, is a not-for-profit organization which offers showings of classic, foreign and avant-garde films, sometimes combined with lectures. It follows a long tradition, begun with silent movies first shown in the room above the old firehouse.

Other Educational Institutions

The Cardinal Farley Military Institute, at the former Ellerslie property, became Holy Cross. It is now defunct. The Rhinebeck Country School on the former Dows Foxhollow property is now Day Top.

Cadets from the Cardinal Farley Military Institute at Ellerslie were an important part of every Memorial Day parade from the founding in 1946 until it was disbanded in 1971. Asher Collection.

The Rhinebeck Performing Arts Center is located three miles east of the village. A temporary tent theater was used to present summer sessions of theatre, dance, music and workshops before the present structure was built in 1998. Photo by Douglas Baz.

Chapter 20
FOCUS ON RELIGION

*t*oday there are six churches within the village of Rhinebeck and four beyond it in the town. When the congregations were new, they held their services in barns, homes, public buildings, or in the churches of other faiths. As they became more established, they put up their own buildings.

The range of beliefs the churches represent—Roman Catholic, Episcopal, Reformed, Lutheran, Methodist, Baptist, and independent—and the level of tolerance and cooperation between them, has distinguished Rhinebeck from its very beginnings. They all seem to live by the ideals expressed by Rhinebeck's own Reverend John Henry Livingston, Dutch Reformed leader and great-grandson of Judge Beekman, at the Fourth Provincial Congress in 1776:

> *It is proper that all men within this State should believe for themselves and worship God according to the dictates of their consciences without depending upon fellow subjects, sister churches, or even the civil magistrates in religion. This prerogative all men possess, and it is not a new grant or any gift from the State but the natural right and just demand of every rational creature.*[47]

Early Palatine Churches

The earliest church in Rhinebeck and probably Dutchess County, was the log building used jointly by the German Reformed and Lutheran congregations of the German Palatine settlers. This church was near Wey's Crossing on Route 9, (the area originally called Rhinebeck), and was used for services of both congregations until 1730 when the Lutherans built a log church where the Old Stone Church now stands.

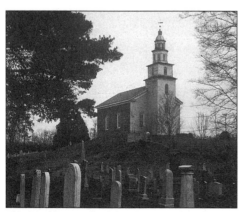

This view of the Stone Church from the cemetery shows the west or back side of the church. It was constructed in 1786 with a doorway facing the main road. In 1824 the steeple and new entrance were added to the church while the former doorway became a window. Nancy Kelly Collection.

The German Reformed congregation continued to use the first log structure until it was damaged in a storm and the congregation decided to move to Red Hook. The church in Red Hook was known as the Zion German Reformed until it became St. Paul's Lutheran Church.

In 1730, the Lutheran congregation built a log church on the site of the present Old Stone Church. It was used until 1786 when the present church was constructed surrounding the log structure. When the stone church was completed, with an entrance facing the main road, the log structure was dismantled. Later, the bell tower was built and church entrance changed to a vestibule at the base of the tower. The church, known as St. Peter's Evangelical Lutheran Church, was the mother church of the other Rhinebeck Lutheran churches. It ceased to have regular services in the 1930s, but has been maintained by the trustees and the cemetery association.

Rhinebeck Dutch Reformed Church

The first church in the present village of Rhinebeck was the Dutch Reformed. The congregation organized in 1729 and built a church in 1732 (the original structure was replaced by the present one in 1809).

The Methodists

Methodism was brought to Rhinebeck by the Rev. Freeborn Garrettson who married Catherine Livingston.

The first Methodist church was built several miles east of the village in 1793 on land which the Garrettsons owned. About ten years later, the church was moved to Center Street in the village. A subsequent stone structure was built at the current location on East Market Street in 1822. The church, a Greek Revival style remained until 1899 when it burned; the present church was constructed the following year.

Two sides of the Rhinebeck Dutch Reformed Church are of brick, while the other two sides are of stone. This unusual arrangement was the result of a compromise during planning for the building. Wealthy members of the congregation contributed money for the bricks while others brought stone for the construction. Asher Collection.

Tommy O'Brien house. The first Methodist service in the village took place at this house on Mill Street which was then the King's Highway. Asher Collection.

The Baptists

The Baptist Church was founded in 1821 by Robert Scott and the first building was begun in 1824. It still stands as the northern most part of the structure which now houses a restaurant at the corner of Livingston and Montgomery Street.

The interior of the Methodist Church (built in 1822) as remodeled by the work of Henry Latson. This building burned in 1899 along with an extensive library including many church records. Museum of Rhinebeck History.

Rhinebeck Methodist Episcopal Church built in 1900. The congregation was founded about 1793. Asher Collection.

Later Village Churches

Village churches built in the first half of the 19th century included the Third Lutheran Church in 1842, and the Episcopal Church of the Messiah in 1852—the structure now used by the Catholic Church of the Good Shepherd.

The strong tradition of cooperation between Rhinebeck churches is evidenced in many ways. During the organization of a new church or after a disastrous fire, other denominations have generously offered their buildings for services. Congregations also have offered their support in fellowship. For example, the Reformed Church's hand-pumped 1845 Backus organ was given to the St. Peter's Lutheran congregation at the Stone Church.

Churches Outside the Village

Outside the village, the Lutheran congregation built a church in Wurtemberg in 1760. The present structure was constructed in 1802. In Rock City, at the eastern edge of the town, the Memorial Lutheran Church was built in 1868.

Rhinebeck Baptist Church is now located in this modern building (circa 1974) on Astor Drive and Montgomery Street. Photo by Douglas Baz.

Third Lutheran Church, on Livingston Street, was built in 1842 and incurred heavy damage from a fire in 1899 but was rebuilt in much the same Greek Revival style. It originally was affiliated with a congregation in Wurtemburg and later with one in Rock City but has had a separate minister for much of its history. Quitman Resource Center National Register Survey.

Good Shepherd Church This structure was built in 1852 for the Episcopal congregation and acquired by the Catholic Archdiocese in 1901. As originally designed by local architect, George Veitch, the church is pictured with the entrance on Mulberry Street. Rokeby Collection.

Church of the Messiah. The original Episcopal congregation organized in 1846 and first built the 1852 structure on East Market Street, now owned by the Catholic Archdiocese. The present stone structure, built in 1896 on Montgomery Street, has been known as the "Millionaire's Church" because the Astors and Mortons were great benefactors of the church. It is adorned with a pipe organ and magnificent stained glass windows. Asher Collection.

Other churches, all now defunct, were the Hillside Methodist Chapel, south of the village on Route 9; the Mt. Rutsen Methodist chapel at Ferncliff Forest; and in Rhinecliff, the Riverside Methodist Church and The Church of the Ascension (an Episcopal church). Hillside M.E. and Riverside had one pastor thru 1888. In 1888, Hillside was joined with Staatsburgh. Riverside was probably united with Rhinebeck. Later Hillside was affiliated with Rhinebeck and recently joined with Rhinebeck, closing the Hillside church.

German settlers in the southeastern part of Rhinebeck organized St. Paul's Lutheran Church in Wurtemburg. A year later, they built a structure on this site. The present building was constructed in 1802. Asher Collection.

Memorial Lutheran Church, built in 1868, was organized through the efforts of John G. Schultz who contributed the land and many of the building materials to support the congregation in Rock City. Quitman Resource Center National Register Survey.

Hillside Methodist, which was founded by Julia Lynch Olin in 1855, is now occupied by an antiques dealer. Dows Collection.

St. Joseph's Catholic Church, Rhinecliff was founded by Father Michael Scully. It was designed by George Veitch and erected in 1864. Quitman Resource Center National Register Survey.

Riverside Methodist Church was built in 1855 in Rhinecliff. In 1973, the congregation joined with Rhinebeck, and the building is now a residence. Quitman Resource Center National Register Survey.

The Church of the Ascension, an Episcopal church, was organized 1858, and built 1871 on Dutchess Terrace, overlooking the river in Rhinecliff. The building burned and ruins are now used as a garden. Asher Collection.

Rhinecliff, Earliest Catholic Church

The first Catholic Church, located in Rhinecliff, was St. Joseph's, built in 1864 through the efforts of Father Michael Scully. It served the many Irish Catholic families that came to town to work on the railroad. The Episcopal church on East Market Street was sold to the Catholics in 1901 for their Rhinebeck congregation when the present Episcopal church, the Church of the Messiah, was built on Montgomery Street.

Grace Bible Fellowship Church

The most recent congregation established in the town is the Grace Bible Fellowship Church, a non-denominational Christian church which now uses the historic Stone Church building north of the village. They are developing plans for a new structure to be located south of the Stone Church cemetery.

Union Tent Meeting This tent meeting held in 1915 featured Evangelist Gypsy Smith. He is shown at left with Reverend Boomhower from Wurtemburg, Reverend Miller from the Rhinebeck Third Lutheran church, Reverend Bennett from the Methodist church and Reverend Ingersoll from the Baptist Church, unnamed pianist and counsellor and a child of Gypsy Smith. Museum of Rhinebeck History.

Twentieth Century Cooperation

The tradition of Unity Services,—joint services held in various village churches, especially during the Season of Lent—has continued for over a century, possibly since the founding of the village. Ministers from the various denominations participate in the service and the Rhinebeck Ministerium prepares the schedule.

This hand pumped organ was constructed by A. B. Backus in 1845 and orginally housed at the Rhinebeck Reformed Church. It is now at the old Stone Church on Route 9. It has been restored but not mechanized. Quitman Resource Center National Register Survey.

Chapter 21
HEALTH CARE

*t*he earliest doctor in Rhinebeck may have come with the Palatine settlers. Later, during the colonial period, Dr. Hans Kiersted, Dr. Ananias Cooper and others ministered to the town's sick.

Thompson Trust

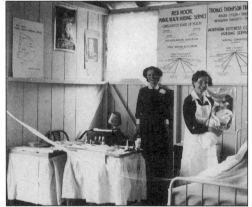

This exhibit at the Dutchess County Fair, circa1945, stressed the benefits of public health care provided with the support of the Thomas Thompson Trust. Asher Collection.

Thomas Thompson and his wife were impressed by the thoughtfulness of a Rhinebeck seamstress, Ina Quick, whom they met on a trip from Brattleboro Vermont, to New York City in 1867. The meeting had a profound effect on Thompson. When he died, he left a large part of his estate in a trust to be used "toward the relief and support of poor seamstresses, needlewomen, and shop girls who may be in temporary need from want of employment, sickness or misfortune in the Towns of Brattleboro, Vermont, and Rhinebeck, Dutchess County, New York." Any excess once the seamstresses and shop girls were cared for was to be used "for the immediate relief of the suddenly needy, whether from casualty, imprudence or improvidence."[48] the benefits of the trust have since been expanded to provide funding for general health care, library facilities, and other projects to benefit the community.

The Thompson House

A 1897 photo of the Thompson House on Livingston Street that served elderly local women. It became an infirmary and the Thompson House Community Center with hospital and nursing services. Rhinebeck Historical Society.

By the time the trust went into effect, there were few needy seamstresses in town. Therefore the monies were used for nursing services and to open a home, the Thompson House on Livingston Street, for elderly local women needing care. The home soon was turned into an infirmary, the Thompson House Community Center, which offered hospital and nursing services. The building next door was purchased for the elderly ladies.

Northern Dutchess Health Center

When the expenses of the center exceeded its resources from the trust, the Northern Dutchess Health Service Center was founded. Together with the Rhinebeck Realty and Development Company, the Thompson Trust collected and donated funds for a new building for the Health Service Center. The building, which became the Northern Dutchess Hospital, was completed in 1930.

Northern Dutchess Hospital

The Hospital was expanded in 1960, raising the total capacity to 72 beds. A new three story wing was added along with interior renovations. Since then, the intensive care unit and medical history library were added. Under the administration of Michael Mazzarella, the hospital has become a 286 bed facility

Northern Dutchess Health Center was dedicated in 1930. It later became the Northern Dutchess Hospital with major additions changing this facade. Since 1999 the hospital has been affiliated with Vassar Hospital in Poughkeepsie. Museum of Rhinebeck History.

and the first hospital-based single-room birth center in New York State.

The Thompson House extended care nursing facility was completed in 1997 on the grounds of the Northern Dutchess Hospital. It is partially funded through the Thompson Trust and the name perpetuates that of Rhinebeck's first hospital facility. Photo by Douglas Baz.

The New Thompson House

Completed in 1977 by the Baptist Home of Brooklyn, the Baptist Home at Brookmeade provides nursing home care for approximately 120 residents, continuing the tradition begun by the home in Brooklyn in 1869. It is located on 74 acres east of the village and is currently a skilled nursing facility. Photo by Douglas Baz.

The Baptist Home

Located on the grounds of the former Astor Estate on River Road, the Ferncliff Nursing Facility is managed by the Carmelite Sisters of the Catholic Church. It opened in 1973. Photo by Douglas Baz.

Ferncliff Nursing Home

Chapter 22
PRESERVATION AND CONSERVATION

*t*he people of Rhinebeck have become acutely aware of the need to conserve their lands, waters, and wildlife and to preserve their history and its traces. Many citizens such as Dewitt Gurnell, Marilyn Hatch, Sally Mazzarella, Kay Verrilli, and Richard Crowley have recognized the importance of preservation and done much to further the preservation movement in town.

Daughters of the American Revolution (DAR)

The Chancellor Livingston Chapter of the National Society of Daughters of the American Revolution was founded in Rhinebeck in 1917 by Helen Delaporte and 27 charter members. The organization seeks to encourage patriotism and preservation. The Chapter has collected pictures and documents; preserved and marked cemeteries; and maintains the historic Montgomery home as its chapter house.

Rhinebeck Historical Society

Founded in 1967, through the efforts of Dewitt Gurnell, the society seeks to perserve the historic character of the village and town of Rhinebeck. The society collects, arranges and cares for historic records that bear on local life of the past. It provides educational programs and a newsletter of historical information.

The gate at the Rhinebeck Cemetery Association on Route 9 in Rhinebeck was dedicated by the DAR, July 4, 1926, in memory of those who served in the military. DAR

Hudson River Heritage

Hudson River Heritage, a non-profit organization, obtained National Historic Landmark status for a stretch of land along the east riverbank on which the 30 or so country seats were built. The group promotes awareness of the landmark district and provides protective support. In addition to the river places, the National Register of Historic Places lists a number of other Rhinebeck buildings and sites, including Delamater House, the Stone Church, and over 400 buildings in the village district.

Hudson River Heritage is a nonprofit membership organization which works as a source of information and protective support for the National Historic Landmark District. Quitman Resource Center National Register Survey.

The Quitman House, on Route 9 north of the Stone Church, was built in 1798 for the Reverend Frederick Quitman by the congregation of St. Peter's Lutheran Church. It was restored by the Quitman Resource Center, which has a perpetual lease for the property from the town of Rhinebeck. The Museum of Rhinebeck History, the Consortium of Rhinebeck History and offices of historic and preservation organizations are housed in the building. Quitman Resource Center National Register Survey.

In 1964, Homer Staley made the arrangements for the gift of Ferncliff Forest from Brooke Astor who donated the land in memory of her husband, Vincent Astor. This preserve is available for hiking and picnics. Homer, a familiar Rhinebeck figure, was the "forest ranger" until his death in 1995. Valerie Kilmer Collection.

CERTIFICATE.

This is to Certify that the Bearer, *John H. Traver* is one of the RIDERS of the RHINEBECK, HYDE PARK AND CLINTON ASSOCIATION FOR THE DETECTION OF HORSE THIEVES, and that any assistance or credit he may ask for while in pursuit of a horse-thief the Society will be responsible for.

Dated at *Rhinebeck* this *1st* day of *Jan'y* 185*7*

Jacob H. Ackert President,

Stephen Lossing Vice. President.

Abraham LeRoy Secretary

The Rhinebeck Society for the Apprehension of Horse Thieves was active from 1850 to 1920. This certificate of membership for John H. Traver is dated January 1, 1857. Museum of Rhinebeck History.

Wilderstein Preservation

Wilderstein Preservation was established in 1980 to restore and preserve the Suckley Estate, to catalogue and preserve the archives and furnishings, and to open the house and grounds to public viewing.

The Quitman Resource Center

The Quitman Resource Center for Preservation was founded in 1974 by members of the Historical Society to rescue the old parsonage of the Stone Church. Today the building houses the Museum of Rhinebeck History and the offices of several organizations for preservation and land conservation.

Winnakee Land Trust

The Winnakee Land Trust, dedicated to enhancing land use and conserving resources, accepts conservation easements, maintains trails, and manages donations of lands. A notable conservation organization, Scenic Hudson, Inc., purchased Burger Hill on Route 9G, overlooking a panorama of the Catskills and the Taconics. Scenic Hudson is assisted by the Winnakee Land Trust in maintaining the property and trails.

Southlands Foundation

The Southlands Foundation, started in 1984, administers a trust endowed by Deborah Dows to preserve the open space of Southlands Farm, once part of the original Beekman patent.

Landsmans Kill Trail Association

The Landsmans Kill Trail Association, established in 1968, supervises a private network of trails and bridle paths for horseback riding made available by landowners in Rhinebeck, Red Hook, and Staatsburgh.

Ferncliff Forest Preserve

The Ferncliff Forest Preserve on Mt. Rutsen Road was created in the interests of preservation and to provide hiking trails and picnic areas. The land was donated by Brooke Astor to Rhinebeck's Rotary Club.

In 1967, the Honorable Dewitt Gurnell assembled interested residents of Rhinebeck to discuss the formation of a historical society. At that time, someone proposed that an appropriate Rhinebeck coat of arms should be developed. At a later meeting, two designs, remarkably similar in concept were presented: one by Arthur C. M. Kelly and the other by Fred Hatesaul. Since Kelly's proposal was in color, the group chose it.

The shield is designed to represent and commemorate the events in the early history of the town. The upper left and lower right corners are representations of the British and Dutch flags and symbolize the early founders of the area. The upper right segment contains a stylized water wheel, which indicates the reliance early settlers had on this form of energy. The lower left pays tribute to the violet industry that played a significant part in Rhinebeck industry. Above the shield, the motto "Ex His Initium" was added to mean "from these beginnings."

Some years later, the town wished to adopt a variation of this seal as their official crest. Gurnell went to the local high school and offered a contest to students. Richard McKibben developed the current town seal, which incorporates the society's seal, overlain with the arms of the Count Palatine of the Rhine Valley in Germany, honoring the 1710 Palatine immigrant families that settled in Rhinebeck at the suggestion of Henry Beekman.

Chapter 23
CONCLUSION

*b*y now, most of the farms have been sold off, the wealth and influence of the river families has diminished, and many of their estates have either been broken up or converted for public use. Other estates, along with some village landmarks, have fallen to ruin or been demolished. Still there remain Dutch barns and stone houses, colonial cottages, and Victorian homes to be protected through preservation efforts.

John Pottenburgh's tombstone in the old Rhinebeck Cemetery contains the inscription:
"Death is a debt to nature due,
Which I have paid and so must you."
John was a Revolutionary War soldier who died November 21, 1819, aged 70 years. Photo by Douglas Baz.

Likewise the importance of agriculture in Rhinebeck has lessened, while the desire to maintain a rural landscape remains strong. This desire has fostered careful and comprehensive planning and zoning regulation, as well as efforts to implement open space conservation.

At the turn of the millennium, here in this place, where the Hudson River flows at its doorstep and the Catskills provide the backdrop as they have through the centuries, we maintain our community and honor its past by preparing for its future.

NOTES

1. Kraft, Herbert C., *The Lenape or Delaware Indians* (New Jersey: Seton Hall University Museum, 1996, 26.
2. E. Smith, *History of Kipsbergen* (New York: The Office of the Rhinebeck Gazette, 1894)
3. Smith, George A., book review: *Stories of the Hudson* (Washington Irving), Hudson Valley Regional Review 2, no. 2 (1985): 75.
4. Gehring, Charles T., and Starna, William A., *Dutch and Indians in the Hudson Valley: The Early Period,* Hudson Valley Regional Review 9, no. 2 (1992): 5–6.
5. Undated article from Rhinebeck Gazette.
6. *Edward Livingston Papers,* C0280, Box 129, Rent Book A (#2), Firestone Library, Princeton University.
7. Rhinebeck Gazette, March 31, 1868.
8. Map 2017, New York State Library manuscripts, Nov. 22, 1786, H. L., Tract Granted Gysbert Westphael and Company, May 1, 1719, and is Called Sepascoot.
9. Morgan Lewis Map, Wittenburgh Tract, 1804 Rhinebeck Historical Society
10. Book of the Supervisors, Old Miscellaneous Records of Dutchess County (New York: Vassar Brothers Institute, 1911), Liber C: 21, 24, 38.
11. Morse, Howard H., *Historic Old Rhinebeck* (New York: by the author, 1908), 70.
12. Falatko, Stephen, "Greek Revival Architecture on the Salisbury Turnpike," Hudson Valley Magazine, October 1993.
13. Wiles, Richard T., ed., *The Livingston Legacy: Three Centuries of American History* (Annandale-on-Hudson: Bard College/Hudson Valley Studies Program, and the New York State Office of Parks, Recreation, & Historic Preervation, Taconic Region, 1986), 70.
14. McDermott, *William P., Knowing One's Place: Leadership and status in Colonial Rhinebeck,* Dutchess County, Hudson Valley Regional Review 15, no. 2 (1998): 62
15. Kierner, Cynthia A., *From Entrepreneurs to Ornaments: The Livingston Women, 1679-1790,* Hudson Valley Regional Review 4, no. 1 (1987): 41.
16. Callaghan, E.B., *Documentary History of New York, Census of 1755, Volume III,* 851.
17. Letter from Gappy Van Vradenburgh to George Shumaker, 1790, Shook Private Collection, copies at Rhinebeck Museum of History.
18. McDermott, William P., *Slavery in Rhinebeck,* NY 1714-1800, Sept 1996, Vol 13, No. 2
19. Morse, Howard H., op. cit., 351.
20. D.A.R., Collection of Town Records of Rhinebeck, Starr Library.
21. Wiles, Richard T., *The Livingston Legacy: Three Centuries of American History* (New York: Bard College/Hudson Valley Studies Program, Notes from Symposium, June 6-7, 1986), 87.
22. Smith, DeCost, *Martyrs of The Oblong and Little Nine* (Idaho: Caxton Printers, Ltd., 1948), 26.
23. Hasbrouck, *The History of Dutchess County, New York* (New York: S. A. Matthieu, 1909), 109.
24. Letter from Richard Montgomery to Janet Montgomery, December 10, 1775, Collection of the DAR, Chancellor Livingston Chapter.
25. When Livingston Manor was first established, a small portion of its lands fell within the boundary of Rhinebeck Precinct, Dutchess County. Robert Livingston built Aryll House south of Clermont and within the bounds of Rhinebeck. The county lines were redefined in 1799 for the sole purpose of keeping all the Livingston property, including Clermont, together in Columbia County.
26. Roosevelt, Franklin D., Events on Hudson's River in 1777, from records of the British Admiralty, Year Book of the Dutchess County Historical Society, 1935, Vol 20, 100.
27. Wermuth, Thomas S., *Economic Opportunity and Moral Economy in the Hudson River Valley During the American Revolution,* Hudson Valley Regional Review 14, no. 2 (1997): 14.
28. Melancton Smith as quoted by Lynd, Staughton, Anti-Federalism in Dutchess County, New York (Illinois: Loyola University Press, 1962), 84
29. Smith, George A., book review: "Bicentennial Minutes: New York's Role in the Ratification of the Constitution" (Daniel M. Kittay, ed.), Hudson Valley Regional Review 6, no. 2 (1989): 103.

30. Blanchard, Frank D., *History of the Reformed Dutch Church of Rhinebeck Flatts, NY* (New York: J. B. Lyon Company, 1931), 1.

31. Morse, Howard H., op. cit., 104.

32. Map of the Wittemburgh Tract Drawn for Morgan Lewis, 1802, Collection of the Rhinebeck Historical Society

33. Letter from Cornelia Morton to Philip J. Schyuler, July 11, 1804, as quoted in Dutchess County Historical Society Yearbook.

34. National Register of Historic Places (Washington, D. C.: United States Department of the Interior, National Park Service), Section 8:2, 9.

35. Blum, John M., Catton, Bruce, Morgan, Edmund S, Schlesinger, Arthur M., Jr., Stampp, Kenneth M., and Woodward, C. Vann, *The National Experience* (New York: Harcourt, Brace & World, Inc., 1963), 198.

36. Clark, Geoffrey. *The Stevens Legacy,* Stevens Humanities Department, www.stevens-tech.edu.

37. Gazette Aug 7, 1873, "R&C Railroad construction to be finished by Sept., 44,000 Tons of Iron Arrived at Slate Dock on Monday."

38. Smith, George A., book review: *America's Iceman* (Joseph C. Jones, Jr.,), Hudson Valley Regional Review 3, no. 1 (1986): 123.

39. Ibid: 125.

40. Museum of Rhinebeck History publication, "Rhinebeck in the Civil War," by Kenneth Burke and Felix Scardapane 1995

41. Rhinebeck Gazette, November 22, 1884.

42. Henry Noble McCracken as quoted in Verrilli, Kay, Violet Notes (New York: Museum of Rhinebeck History, 1997), 11.

43. Tietjen, Sari B., *Rhinebeck: Portrait of a Town* (New York: Phanter Press, 1990), 68.

44. U.S. Federal Census 1910 and 1930, (Rhinebeck, County of Dutchess, New York State).

45. Blum, John M., et. al., op. cit., 699.

46. Verrilli, Kay T., World War II, Military, Home Front, 2000 Exhibit, Museum of Rhinebeck History, also American Legion Post and Memorial Plaques at the Rhinebeck Fire House.

47. Lawrence, Thea, *Unity Without Uniformity: An Exploration into the History of the Churches of Rhinebeck, NY,* Hudson Valley Regional Review 1, no. 2 (1984): 105.

48. Tietjen, Sari B., op. cit., 108.

BIBLIOGRAPHY

Books

Cook, S.G., MD and Charles Benton. *The Dutchess County Regiment in the Civil War,* Danbury CT, Medical printing Co, 1907.

Dixon, Nancy Wagoner. *Palatine Roots,* Camden ME, Picton Press, 1994.

Dows, Olin. *Franklin Roosevelt at Hyde Park,* New York, American Artist Group, 1949.

Dutchess County Planning Board. *Landmarks of Dutchess County,* New York State Council on the Arts, 1969.

Hasbrouck, Frank. *The History of Dutchess County New York,* Poughkeepsie, NY, S.A. Matthieu, 1909.

Jones, Henry Z Jones, Jr. *The Palatine Families of New York, A Study of the German Immigrants Who Arrived in Colonial New York in 1710, 2 Volumes,* Universal City CA, 1985.

Jones, Henry Z Jones, Jr. *More Palatine Families,* Universal City Ca, 1991.

Kelly, Arthur C.M. *Baptism Record of Eight Episcopal Congregations of Old Rhinebeck, New York 1816–1899,* Rhinebeck NY, Kinship, 1972.

———. *Baptism Record of Reformed Church, Rhinebeck, New York 1731–1899,* Rhinebeck NY, Kinship, 1970.

———. *Baptism Record of St. Peter's Lutheran Church, Rhinebeck, New York 1733–1899,* Rhinebeck NY, Kinship, 1968.

———. *Baptism Record of St. Paul's Lutheran Church of Wurtemburg, Rhinebeck, New York 1760–1899,* Rhinebeck NY, Kinship, 1969.

———. *Baptism Record of St. Paul's (Zion's) Lutheran Church, Red Hook, New York 1730–1899,* also called *German Reformed Zion's Church of Rhinebeck,* Rhinebeck NY, Kinship, 1971.

———. *Marriage Record of The Four Reformed Congregations of Old Rhinebeck, Dutchess County, New York 1731–1899,* Rhinebeck NY, Kinship, 1971.

———. *Marriage Record of Three Lutheran Congregations of, Rhinebeck, New York 1746–1899,* Rhinebeck NY, Kinship, 1969

———. *Rhinebeck, New York Death Records of the 18th and 19th Centuries,* Rhinebeck NY, Kinship, 1992.

———. *Deaths, Marriages and Much Miscellaneous from Rhinebeck New York Newspapers 1846–1899, 2 Volumes,* Rhinebeck NY, Kinship, 1978.

———. *Dutchess County, NY Probate Records 1787–1865,* Rhinebeck NY, Kinship, 1997

———. *Rhinebeck Precinct Account Book 1783–1788,* Rhinebeck NY Kinship, 1999.

———. *Peter J. Schultz Account Book 1724–1746,* Rhinebeck NY, Kinship, 1999.

———. *Vital Records of the Reformed Churches of Upper Red Hook, Tivoli, etc.1766–1899,* Rhinebeck NY, Kinship, 1973.

Kim, Sun Bok. *Landlord and Tenant in Colonial New York Manorial Society 1664–1775,* Chapel Hill NC, 1978

Koehler, Linda, *Dutchess County, New York Churches and Their Records: An Historical Directory,* Rhinebeck NY, Kinship, 1994.

Lawrence, Thea. *Unity Without Uniformity, the Rhinebeck Church Community 1718–1918,* Monroe NY, Library Research Associates, 1992.

Lynd, Staughton. *Anti-Federalism in Dutchess County, New York,* Chicago IL, Loyola U.,1962.

MacCracken, Henry Noble. *Blithe Dutchess,* New York, Hastings House, 1958.

———. *Old Dutchess Forever,* New York, Hastings House, 1956.

McElroy, Robert. *Levi Parsons Morton: Banker, Diplomat and Statesman,* New York, G.P. Putnam's Sons, 1930.

Morse, Howard H. *Historic Old Rhinebeck,* Rhinebeck, NY, 1908.

Nowell, Elizabeth. *Thomas Wolfe,* New York, Doubleday & Co., 1960.

O'Callaghan, Edmund. *Documentary History of New York State, 4 Volumes,* New York, Albany 1849

———. *Documents Relative to the Colonial History of the State of New York, 15 Volumes,* New York, Albany 1853–1887.

Power, John Carroll. *Abraham Lincoln, His Great Funeral Cortege,* Springfield, Ill., 1872.

Reynolds, Helen Wilkinson. *Dutchess County Doorways,* New York, W.F. Payson, 1931.

Seabrook, William B. *Those Foreigners,* New York, Harcourt, Brace, 1958.

Smith, DeCost. *Martyrs of The Oblong and Little Nine,* Caldwell, ID, Caxton Printers, 1948.

Smith, Edward M. *History of Kipsbergen Rhinebeck, NY (1894),* Rhinebeck NY, Kinship 1992.

Smith, Edward M. *Documentary History of Rhinebeck, in Dutchess County, NY.* Rhinebeck, NY.: 1881.

Smith, James. *History of Duchess County New York, with Illustrations 1683–1882,* Poughkeepsie 1882.

Smith, Philip H. *General History of Duchess County, from 1609–1876, Inclusive,* Pawling NY, 1877.

Tietjen, Sari B. *Rhinebeck, Portrait of a Town, Rhinebeck,* New York, Phanter Press, 1990.

Ward, Geoffrey. *Closest Companion, Letters of FDR and Margaret Suckley,* 1996

Wharton, Edith. *The Age of Innocence,* New York, D. Appleton & Co., 1920.

———. *Hudson River Bracketed,* New York, D. Appleton & Co., 1929.

Wiles, Richard T. *The Livingston Legacy, Three Centuries of American History,* Annandale NY, Bard College, 1987.

Wolfe, Thomas. *Of Time and the River,* New York, Charles Scribners' Sons, 1935.

———. *Commemorative Biographical Review of Dutchess County,* New York, Chicago, J.H. Beers & Co., 1897.

———. *Dutchess County: American Guide Series,* Philadelphia PA, William Penn Association of Philadelphia, 1937.

Newspapers, Periodicals and Booklets

"A Walking Tour of Rhinebeck," New York, Rhinebeck Historical Society, 1973.

"A Work for An Entire Community," Rhinecliff Memorial Building, 1910.

"Rhinebeck Savings Bank," 1860-1960.

Babbitt, Katherine M. "Janet Montgomery: Hudson River Squire," Monroe NY, Library Research Associates, 1975.

"Dutchess County Genealogical Society," The Dutchess, quarterly published 1973–.

"Dutchess County Historical Society," The Yearbook, published annually, 1914–.

Dows, Olin, et al. "Murals in the Rhinebeck Post Office," Rhinebeck, NY, 1940

Gurnell, Dewitt. "A Condensed History of Rhinebeck with Tour Routes," Rhinebeck, NY, 1973.

Gurnell, Dewitt. "Rhinebeck During the Revolutionary War," Rhinebeck, NY 1975.

Hughes, J. Theodore. "An Historical Sketch of the Life of Freeborn Garrettson," Pioneer Methodist Preacher, Rutland VT, 1984

The Hudson Valley Regional Review

March 1984, Vol 1, No.1 "Patrons and the patronized: The Case of Maria James" William Wilson

Sept. 1986, Vol 3, No. 2 "Colonial Land Grants in Dutchess County, NY" William P. McDermott

Sept. 1989, Vol. 6, No. 2 "Rhinebeck: Transition in 1799" Nancy V. Kelly

Sept. 1990, Vol. 7, No. 2 "Wilderstein: The Creation of a Hudson River Villa, 1852–1897" Cynthia O. Philip

Sept. 1991, Vol 8, No. 2 "Henry James as a Small Boy in Rhinebeck" William Wilson

March 1994, Vol 11, No. 1 "Experience and Innocence in Rhinebeck" Edith Wharton

Sept. 1996, Vol 13, No. 2 "Slavery in Rhinebeck, NY 1714–1800" William P. McDermott

Historical Maps

c.1737 First Division of Henry Beekman's Land

1769 William Traphagen conveyance by Charles DeWitt (Livingston Collection)

1786 Sepascoot Tract and lands of William VanVredenburg by NYSL Albany-Manuscripts

1798 Alexander Thompson Map 3 versions, originals at Starr Library, NYSL Albany-Manuscripts, and Princeton Library- Livingston Collection

1802 Ulster and Salisbury Turnpike Maps, Dutchess County Clerk's Office and NYSL Albany-Manuscripts

1803 Robert Gilbert Livingston's Land by Alexander (Livingston Collection)

1803 property of Janet Montgomery surveyed 1804, copied by John Cox Jr. 1804 (Livingston Collection)

1804 Morgan Lewis Map, Wittenburgh Tract, Rhinebeck Historical Society

1840 Burr Map (no houses) - NYSL Albany- Manuscripts

1848 Panoramic View by William Wade (D-Fish Library, Putnam Co)

1850 Dutchess County Map with houses

1858 Dutchess County Map with houses

1868 Beer's Atlas, Rhinebeck Town Historian and DAR Collection
1876 Gray Atlas New Historical Atlas of Dutchess County, NY Illustrated, Reading Publishing House, O.W. Gray & son & F.A. Davis, copyright 1876, Adriance Library
1890 Bird's eye View of Village L.R. Burleigh, Troy, NY, Battistoni Office, RHS printed copies
1890-1926 Sanborn Insurance Maps, color coded for building type
1892 New York Atlas (Hudson Valley to Post Road) Adriance Library

Museum of Rhinebeck History
The 128th Regiment, New York Volunteers (U.S. Infantry) 1995
The 150th Regiment, New York Volunteer Infantry 1995
The First World War and Rhinebeck in the 1920's, Kenneth J. Burke 1998
Sweet Violets, Kay Verrilli and others 1997
World War II, Military, Home Front, Kay T. Verrilli, 2000 Exhibit, Museum of Rhinebeck History
Pugsley, S. Velma, Portraits of Dutchess 1680-1807, Poughkeepsie NY, Hamilton Reproductions, 1976.
Rhinebeck Gazette, various issues.
Rhinebeck Historical Society, A Rhinebeck Album, 1776-1876-1976, Rhinebeck NY, Moran Printing, 1976.
The Thomas Wolfe Review, 1985, p 19-25 "Thomas Wolfe and the Hudson River Aristocracy", Rena R. Corey